ATER MANCHESTER

Managing Urban Spaces in Town Centres
Good Practice Guide

UML WITHDRAWN

ATCM

Association of
TOWN CENTRE
MANAGEMENT

a report for the
Association of
Town Centre Management

by

Chesterton
in association with
Pedestrian Market Research Services Ltd

Sponsored by
...the Environment
...rise
...nists
...er

...tionery Office

EPQ0P

Study Team

Project Director: Christina Tomalin, The Bartlett School of Planning,
University College London

Core Team: Peter Wilks, Chesterton
Peter Hawkes, Chesterton
Mark Boxer, Pedestrian Market Research Services Ltd

DoE Nominated Officer: Marion Headicar, Urban Regeneration Division, Department
of the Environment

Steering Group: Dr David Bannister, University College London
Dr Nicholas Falk, URBED (Urban & Economic Development
Group)
John Gould, Scottish Enterprise
Chris Pagdin, Department of the Environment
Marie Pender, Department of the Environment
Alan K. Tallentire, ATCM (Association of Town Centre
Management)
Helen Woolley, The University of Sheffield

Department of the Environment
Eland House
Bressenden Place
London SW1E 5DU

Telephone 0171 890 3000

Association of Town Centre Management
1 Queen Anne's Gate
Westminster
London SW1H 9BT

Tel: 0171 222 0120
Fax: 0171 222 4440

ISBN 0110-753000 0

Foreword

by Nick Raynsford MP
Parliamentary Under Secretary of State (Minister for London and Construction).

I believe that this good practice guide, and the case studies of the design and management of urban spaces it examines, will make a major contribution to the enhancement of our town centres and will help to generate a significant level of investment through public/private sector partnerships. This Guide is a vital tool for all those involved in improving town centres to demonstrate the economic benefits resulting from environmental improvements. Many of the myths that surround pedestrianisation and other urban space enhancements are addressed.

The research undertaken to prepare this Guide has confirmed that well-managed and maintained urban spaces are critical to the success of our town centres, and can provide both social and economic benefits. However, the research has also demonstrated that local authorities must carefully consider the suitability of environmental improvements within the wider context of a town centre's role and structure. Urban space enhancements should not be considered in isolation, but must be only one element of a town centre strategy.

Drawing on examples of best practice, the Guide makes recommendations on the inception, implementation and management of urban space enhancement schemes, and provides strategic guidance on the appropriateness of these schemes to tackle the range of problems that town centres face.

I commend this Guide not only to towns considering urban space enhancements, but also to all those interested in the future prosperity of our town centres. I hope, therefore, that it will be widely read by professionals from all disciplines, property owners, retailers and local people.

The Department and the Association of Town Centre Management are working together to promote vitality and viability in our town centres, and we support the need for effective town centre management through partnerships. The Government is pleased to be identified with the movement to improve our town centres, and to endorse this guide and its companion on town centre partnerships, as a contribution to improving current practice.

CONTENTS

CHAPTER 1

Introduction   8

CHAPTER 2

Understanding Urban Spaces in Town Centres   11

CHAPTER 3

Resolving Conflict: The Pedestrianisation Debate   20

CHAPTER 4

Measuring Success   23

CHAPTER 5

Commercial Success: The Evidence   26

CHAPTER 6

Approach to Implementation   31

CHAPTER 7

Case Study Towns and Schemes   39

      Aberdeen   40
      Ayr   41
      Bournemouth   44
      Bradford   46
      Cardiff   48
      Conwy   50
      Coventry   52
      Darlington   54
      Derby   56
      Elgin   59
      Hemel Hempstead   61
      Ilford   63
      Kilmarnock   65
      Market Harborough   67
      Morecambe   69
      Petersfield   71
      Solihull   73
      Stowmarket   75
      Windsor   77
      Worcester   79

CHAPTER 1
Introduction

Background

The House of Commons Environment Committee inquiry into the future of shopping centres (October 1994) recommended that the Department of the Environment (DoE), local authorities and the Association of Town Centre Management (ATCM) should work together with other interested parties to encourage vitality and viability in town centres, and improve quality for town centre users. The revised Planning Policy Guidance Note 6 "Town Centres and Retail Developments" (June 1996) confirms the Government's support for town centres and emphasises the need for effective town centre management through partnerships. One consequence of this commitment to town centres is the need to improve our understanding of the benefits of strategic planning and management of urban spaces within town centres.

The ATCM, sponsored by the DoE, Scottish Enterprise, Boots the Chemists and Marks & Spencer, commissioned property consultants Chesterton, the Bartlett School of Architecture and Planning in association with Pedestrian Market Research Services, to prepare this Good Practice Guide on the strategic planning and management of urban spaces within town centres. A parallel study report, Town Centre Partnerships, has also been prepared by URBED (Urban & Economic Development Group) for the ATCM and DoE.

OBJECTIVES

Ease of movement is essential in town centres. Successful centres allow visitors to move between attractions without any kind of discomfort. However, many town centres are increasingly dominated by the car. Open areas in the centres of our towns and cities are too often grey spaces which are neglected and under used. The potential exists to transform many of these areas into vibrant, attractive assets of city life. To unlock this potential, many questions must be asked:

- how do people use urban spaces?
- what positive roles do urban spaces play?
- how can urban spaces help to create successful town centres?
- how important are urban spaces to increasing footfall in town centres?
- how can urban spaces be improved and managed effectively?

This good practice guide intends to shed light on these issues and others relating to urban spaces, and to broaden understanding of urban space enhancement and management. It seeks to identify how urban space enhancement schemes have contributed to the success of town centres, using examples to help to establish good practice. The guide focuses upon the:

- interrelationship between people and space: how the planning of space can encourage the use of facilities and improve the visitor's experience;
- key factors which influence the successful management of urban spaces within town centres;
- identification of good practice in the public participation, planning, design and development

and improvement of these spaces;

- different approaches or solutions adopted to meet varying problems; and the
- variety of methods for implementing and encouraging good practice.

This guide does not intend to provide detailed design guidelines, such as specifications for landscape works, pavements (widths etc.), street furniture and materials to be used. However, this guide addresses the key principles which underpin the successful planning and management of urban spaces, and includes examples of strategic solutions.

The good practice guide aims to:

- demonstrate how the benefits of well planned and managed urban spaces can out-weigh additional costs;
- demonstrate the good practice approach which will ensure successful urban spaces;
- provide suitable examples of physical solutions within urban spaces that can be used to address a range of problems;
- highlight current thinking on the subject area and highlight emerging innovations and activities.

SCOPE

The definition of urban spaces within town centres is wide ranging, and includes the following:

- pedestrianised streets or lanes;
- partially pedestrianised streets;
- market or public squares;
- incidental open space (e.g. planting areas); and
- pavements and footpaths.

The study does not encompass town centre parks which have been addressed by the Department of the Environment's Greening the City – A Guide to Good Practice.

METHODOLOGY

This Good Practice Guide is the result of a major research programme, involving three main areas of work:

- a literature review to identify current thinking on successful urban spaces;
- a survey of local authorities who have implemented urban space enhancement schemes; and
- case study appraisals of 20 successful schemes across the country.

The aim of the survey of local authorities was to identify the scale and scope of urban space enhancement schemes undertaken in town centres during the last decade, and to gauge local authorities' views on how successful these schemes have been in their area. The survey generated a large response (285 local authorities).

CASE STUDY SELECTION CRITERIA

Geographical Spread – A selection of projects which are representative of the experience throughout Great Britain.

Type and Size of Town Centre – Projects with an even coverage of shopping centres, including large city centres, market towns, historic towns and tourist resorts.

Nature of Project – A wide range of enhancement schemes designed to tackle a variety of problems.

Date of Completion – Projects implemented during the last 10 years.

Available Information – Projects where evaluation data is available.

Success – Projects which are perceived to have been successful.

Selected Case Study Towns and Cities

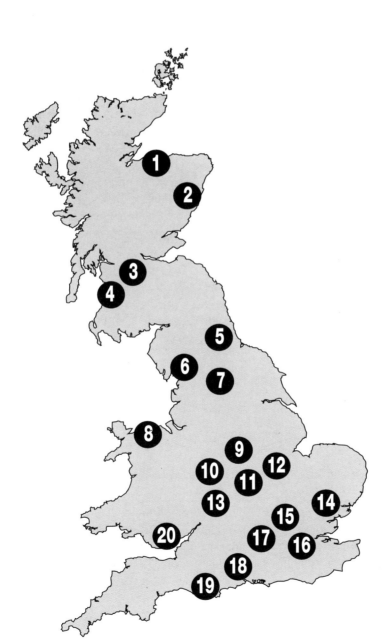

1. Elgin
2. Aberdeen
3. Kilmarnock
4. Ayr
5. Darlington
6. Morecambe
7. Bradford
8. Conwy
9. Derby
10. Coventry
11. Solihull
12. Market Harborough
13. Worcester
14. Stowmarket
15. Hemel Hempstead
16. Ilford
17. Windsor
18. Petersfield
19. Bournemouth
20. Cardiff

CHAPTER 2
Understanding Urban Spaces in Town Centres

The Function of Urban Spaces within Town Centres

Many of the mistakes made within our town centres are due to the lack of understanding about the mix of elements that make outdoor spaces popular. Many urban space improvement schemes have focused on symptoms rather than underlying problems, and have concentrated on cosmetic improvements. In order to identify suitable solutions it is important to understand the historic and present day function of urban spaces.

Public spaces within town centres can be classified into two broad categories: 'links' and 'nodes'. Links are roads, paths, pavements or pedestrianised areas which constitute routes allowing movement between land uses and attractions. Nodes are cross-roads where a number of links meet in the form of public spaces such as market squares or plazas. The primary roles or functions of public spaces (links and nodes) are:

Movement: Urban spaces facilitate the movement of pedestrians and vehicles between land uses and attractions, including shops, services, car parks, residential areas, open spaces and public transport nodes. Successful urban spaces are permeable and encourage freedom of movement. However, this is never easy to achieve for both pedestrians and vehicles.

The balance between integration and segregation of traffic depends on the need for accessibility, and this should be considered carefully (Gehl, 96). Land marks, signing and the overall legibility of the infrastructure all have important roles to play in facilitating movement within town centres. At points of congestion the removal of obstacles and 'clutter' to increase pedestrian capacity are also important.

Focal Point: Public spaces can provide an important focal point for a town centre, which demonstrate to the visitor that they have reached the heart of the town centre. Historic or important buildings need a context and a town square can be an expression of a town's civic pride, historic power and importance (ecclesiastical or administrative).

Solihull High Street

A Market Space: Historically, many public spaces within town centres have provided areas for markets where goods have been displayed and sold. Town centre spaces have also been areas for entertainment, and this role is often important today. Many public areas are used for market stalls which can have an important role in the overall retail mix within a town centre.

A place to meet and rest

The economic impact of market stalls as well as other open space uses (e.g. street entertainment, exhibitions) is important. In addition, it is important to recognise that market stalls add to the display opportunities within a town centre and provide a visual, accessible focus of activity for all visitors. Shop frontages, window displays and market stalls all contribute to the market space within a town centre.

A Place to Meet: Public spaces have an important social and cultural function, providing the public with places to meet, rest or stop and talk. These 'optional' activities take place only when outdoor areas are of high quality. These spaces invite the visitor to stop and interrupt more 'essential' activities such as shopping, or going to work or school.

Parking and Servicing: Increasingly, public spaces have become areas where visitors can park their cars or where delivery vehicles can access commercial premises.

CONFLICTING ROLES

The roles and functions of urban spaces, as highlighted above, are in many cases contradictory as well as complementary. For example, a requirement for ease of movement can conflict with parking and servicing requirements where stationary vehicles present a physical barrier to pedestrian movement. The successful management of space requires a balance to be struck between each role based upon an understanding of the important interrelationships between each role.

Dr Nicholas Falk (1995) suggests that vitality and viability of a town depends on striking a balance between attractions, accessibility and amenity. This balance will vary between towns. For example, historic towns may successfully exclude traffic from the town centre, whilst other towns may need to retain convenience and accessibility to remain competitive.

Solutions to reduce conflict in urban spaces have concentrated on the following measures.

Space Allocation at Links: Pedestrians and vehicles can be allocated their own spaces in an attempt to separate conflicting users. For example, widening pavements will help to ease pedestrian congestion and "calm" traffic on the highway. The good practice examples demonstrate how priorities for space allocation can be set.

Space Allocation at Nodes: The allocation of space for different uses does not on its own eliminate conflict. Conflict occurs at junctions, for example pedestrians need to cross vehicular streets. In such cases, the physical prioritisation of space for pedestrians is essential to resolve conflict.

Traffic Calming: The introduction of measures to calm traffic is a clear recognition of the conflict that can exist between pedestrians and vehicles. A range of traffic calming measures have been implemented across the country in recent years with varying degrees of success.

Restricted Servicing: Restricted hours for servicing and delivery are often implemented to reduce conflict congestion, noise and pollution.

SUCCESSFUL URBAN SPACES

The importance of well managed and attractive urban spaces within our town centres is widely recognised. There has been a considerable amount of research in recent years relating to the effectiveness of town centre management and possible solutions to spatial problems within town centres. However, little is known about the actual benefits to customers and businesses.

The spaces between buildings are seen as being vital to the success of town centres as a whole, increasing the centres' attraction to shoppers. The social benefits of urban space improvements, in terms of aesthetic quality, reduced congestion, noise and pollution, and the provision of more usable spaces are widely accepted. However, the potential commercial benefits are less well understood. Indeed, many players, including some retailers and investors are sceptical about the importance of well planned and maintained urban spaces in enhancing commercial vitality.

The success of well planned and managed urban spaces can be viewed from four perspectives, that is against the requirements of four primary groups:

- occupiers;
- investors;
- users (customers and visitors); and
- local authorities as developers and managers, and other funding bodies.

OCCUPIERS AND INVESTORS

Success from the occupier's perspective, retailers and other traders, can be measured in terms of higher pedestrian flows and increased trading levels. However, other indicators may be considered important such as improved security, improved access and service arrangements, reduced fly-posting or graffiti. For investors, increased demand for space (improved occupancy rates), higher rental growth, higher capital values and lower yields will constitute success.

Service and delivery requirements are an important consideration for occupiers and need to be addressed when managing open spaces. The conflict between these requirements and shoppers' needs and environmental issues create major difficulties for retailers. Servicing is hampered by:

- local authority restricted delivery times;
- road congestion;
- pedestrianisation and traffic calming measures; and
- other physical constraints, such as narrow streets in historic towns.

Deliveries are often discouraged during the day time, in order to reduce vehicle/pedestrian conflict. The logistic practices of the retailers can help to reduce congestion. The individual circumstances within each town need to be taken into account, and local solutions must be found.

The Square, Market Harborough

St. Nicholas Shopping Centre, Aberdeen

USERS

The measures of success for users or pedestrians are more difficult to quantify. Increased pedestrian flow can be seen as a product of success but this does not identify the components of that success or the user's perceptions of success. From a user's view point, successful urban spaces in town centres can be a combination of the following:

- Pleasant environment
  - design quality
  - ambience
  - reduced congestion/traffic
  - cleanliness and less graffiti etc.
  - low emissions/fumes
  - less noise
  - perceived safety

- Better choice of facilities
  - shops
  - leisure/entertainments
  - community and civic facilities
  - places to eat

- Ease of movement
  - permeability
  - clear sign-posting
  - access for the disabled/elderly/
    people with children
  - pedestrian/vehicle crossings

- Improved accessibility
  - public transport
  - car parks
  - pedestrian routes
  - cycle routes and parking

- Provision of amenities
  - benches and other street furniture
  - places to meet or shelter
  - toilets

- Improved public safety and security.

Finally, local authorities and other funding bodies will view success from a number of perspectives, related to their aims and objectives for the town centre. Ultimately, local authorities will measure success by gauging the level of local support, both from residents and businesses alike, and value for money.

To date there has been little research into successful urban spaces. However, Carmen Hass-Klau (1994) attempted to identify factors which make urban spaces popular, through observations of pedestrian behaviour, pedestrian counts and questionnaire surveys. Five towns in Britain (Brighton, Chichester, Haywards Heath, Horsham and Winchester), three towns in Germany (Esslingen, Luneburg and Starnberg) and three towns in Italy (Como, Saronno and Vicenza) were examined.

The findings of this research suggest that contemporary squares/urban spaces do not attract large numbers of people despite the absence of parked cars and traffic. A number of characteristics were missing from the designs which contributed to the lack of success of the schemes. These missing elements were:

- benches and informal possibilities for sitting and relaxing;

- something to watch, primarily people or water features;

- being on a pedestrian route;

- seeing the full dimension of the square when walking along; and

- having an ambience.

The researchers admitted that they were unable to grade the importance of each characteristic and that the objectivity of some of the characteristics was difficult to explain. However, a number of conclusions reached were potentially useful to the development of urban spaces in Great Britain. These conclusions were:

- modest levels of traffic did not appear to bother people too much when they were sitting in a pedestrianised area;

- the greatest proportion of respondents preferred pedestrianised streets or squares within their town rather than trafficked streets;

- in the British towns, the more compact and integrated the town centre the more people like it;

- large expanses of pedestrianised space can be uninviting; and

- in all the British towns most respondents preferred particular streets and squares because of their atmosphere.

Bearing these factors in mind, the creation of new or enhanced urban spaces for people to meet, rest or spend time needs to be considered carefully. An attractive space with high quality and ample street furniture will not always be successful, in terms of public usage. The accessibility or location of the space is of primary importance. These spaces need to be central to other activities or easily accessible for pedestrians. Ideally, they should be located within the main shopping or employment area, or on a major link to the centre with significant pedestrian flow.

However, a centrally located space can be unsuccessful if it offers little shelter, particularly from the wind. Aesthetic quality of the urban space may be less important than these considerations in attracting users. For example, the public space created on the roof of the St. Nicholas shopping centre in Aberdeen is relatively unattractive but successful, as it offers one of the few sheltered open spaces within the city centre.

USER PERCEPTIONS

The benefits of well designed and managed urban spaces can be measured by; examining users' behaviour, ascertaining the views and opinions of users, or assessing environmental benefits. The assessment of case study towns demonstrates that users' satisfaction with urban space schemes was universally high. User surveys conducted in nine of the case study towns indicated that public satisfaction with enhancement schemes was extremely high. Satisfaction amongst respondents ranged from 70-90% of all users interviewed.

The creation of a new town square in Bournemouth was considered to be successful and a significant improvement by 94% of respondents to a visitor survey.

Traffic calming and environmental enhancement measures implemented in six towns were evaluated as part of the Department of Transport's Bypass

Bournemouth's new town square

Improved pedestrian accessibility – Solihull   High quality design – Mill Lane, Cardiff

Demonstration Project. Public attitude surveys explored opinions on a range of issues after the measures had been implemented. Respondents in all towns recorded very high levels of improvement relating to traffic, parking, noise, pollution, safety and pavement widths.

The attitudes of children are often ignored, despite their importance to the vitality of town centres. Research by the Departments of Landscape and Geography, University of Sheffield examines the attitudes and behaviour of children (aged 9-15) in 14 town centres across the UK. This research project, which was structured around the Futuretown education pack sponsored by Boots The Chemists and Marks and Spencer plc, demonstrates that children are important town centre customers. Over 70% of children visit their town centre once a week or more. The level of litter, traffic, graffiti, vandalism and alcoholics within town centres were highlighted as major concerns amongst children. Better places to meet and more street features (seats, water features) were cited as improvements children would like to see in town centres.

MAINTAINING QUALITY

Customers now expect to see high standards of design and quality within city and town centres. A major issue facing any local authority or town centre management partnership looking to improve public spaces is the need to provide quality on the one hand and to keep costs down on the other. Resources are limited and a very careful balance between costs and quality always needs to be found. Work should be phased where funding is limited, rather than compromising on scheme details. It is essential to achieve suitable quality in design, materials and workmanship and appropriate coverage wherever urban space improvements are implemented.

Good practice must achieve value for money, which will not always mean the cheapest solution. Experienced contractors with a proven track record should be used. Low cost improvements/street furniture and landscaping can look tired and dated fairly quickly, whereas more expensive solutions can last longer and be more cost effective in the long run, as they need to be replaced less frequently. The overall quality of a scheme should match the specific requirements of a given town centre, in particular the overall quality of the streetscape.

GOOD STREET DESIGN

No urban space enhancement scheme can replace good street design in town centres. It is essential that the components and processes needed to achieve high quality streetscapes are transferred across all areas regardless of the agreed level of pedestrian priority. Good street design enables a number of potentially conflicting activities to occur at one time. Highlighting pinch-points can be an effective way to identify and ameliorate conflicts. Examples include – bus stops which hinder the flow of pedestrian traffic, retailers restricting access to the roadway, pedestrians denied proper waiting room at crossings, traffic lights, or other waiting spaces.

The careful use of materials can help to alleviate problems of pedestrian/vehicular conflict and can improve safety. For example, the 'carpeting' of street crossings using ornamental paving design can show where pedestrians have priority and highlight key links. The careful use of materials can also reduce the need for ramps and chicanes to calm traffic.

The methods used for integrating public transport links within town centres are important in good street design. The location, frequency and design of bus stops are critical elements of the management of space in town centres. Ease of movement from public transport nodes to the main retail areas is essential. Bus and railway stations should be designed to provide an attractive face to users.

STREET FURNITURE

Appropriate street furniture can be used to reinforce local identity. Street furniture is a vital part of the streetscape as well as having an important functional role. Commissioning artists to design street furniture and public art can help to ensure that a scheme does not look 'out of a catalogue'. For example, specially designed street furniture was implemented in Ayr town centre and Mill Lane in Cardiff, based on local themes. Public art with a strong local feel has been implemented in many town centres, including Derby and Hemel Hempstead. Flags and banners can also help to make a centre memorable and fun to visit and improve dull facades. The use of lighting at relatively low cost transforms quite ordinary buildings, improving the attraction of the centre during the evening.

Unfortunately, some features intended to attract people can fail. For instance, empty benches, fountains and sculpture which fail to attract, ignored pedestrian crossings or disused cycle parks. These features should be identified and removed or re-sited. Under used facilities present a barrier to the potential of the streetscape. The provision of attractive spaces and street furniture cannot create vitality and viability on their own. These features need to be planned and located with great care. They should not obstruct retail frontages or disrupt pedestrian flow.

The measures implemented in Hemel Hempstead have transformed the town centre into a safer, more attractive environment predominantly for the use of pedestrians. The provision of public art has drawn attention away from the bland 1960s architecture and has provided a clean and modern shopping environment.

Signposting, maps and public art at key points can make the centre more memorable and easier to understand.

Signposting is usually designed and planned by people who are familiar with the town centre. However, strangers to the town may be better judges of appropriate signposting. The views of strangers should be sought during the planning of signposting, or even tested prior to implementation.

Finger-posts in Windsor

ENGINEERING AND URBAN DESIGN SOLUTIONS

Many early urban space enhancement schemes during the 1970s used man-made materials which had a short life. Surviving examples of these early schemes look tired and dated. Many of these schemes were engineering driven, concentrating on the functional requirements of vehicular traffic and the need to segregate pedestrians and traffic. The requirements of the pedestrian and aesthetic quality were often neglected.

In order to be successful projects generally need to contain both aesthetic and engineering solutions. The precise mix between these factors may vary but they are inextricably linked with performance and appearance of the scheme.

The Ayr Traffic Plan and Streetscape Project demonstrate how physical constraints can be overcome through the implementation of design and traffic management. The formation of a joint multi-disciplinary team was critical to the planning and implementation of the scheme, and provided a balance between practical engineering solutions and aesthetic design quality.

MATERIALS AND DURABILITY

The expected lifespan of an enhancement scheme should be considered fully during the planning stage and the choice of materials will be a key consideration. Up-front costs are often a key feature constraining the project. A short-termism view in the use of cheaper materials may disadvantage the life cycle costs of the scheme. Where possible, looking to the longer term should be encouraged and promoted by the use of quality materials in keeping with the local natural and built environment. In particular the costs of different materials and their expected durability/lifespan must be assessed. This assessment should not only consider the cost of materials versus life expectancy, but also the potential on-going maintenance, management and cleaning costs associated with each solution. The future maintenance and cleaning regime must be linked to the chosen design solution.

In relatively modern town centres with little historic character, it is necessary to bear in mind the rapid changes within the retail market. Therefore, the use of lower quality but cheaper materials can provide the opportunity for the local authority to keep up with changing design fashions through regular renewal. Regular renewal allows local authorities to remove worn out and dated features and to keep ahead of local competition. However, regular renewal can be disruptive and unpopular with the public and traders. Politically it can also be unacceptable, as it can be seen as a waste of public funds. Therefore, schemes should always be relatively durable, and should last at least 10-15 years.

Within centres which have a prominent historic character, it may be more appropriate to use more durable and expensive materials. The use of natural and local materials is less likely to become unfashionable and usually has a longer lifespan. The aesthetic quality of natural materials tends to improve with age, and these materials are less prone to weathering and staining. Weathering can improve the look of natural materials, whilst man-made materials are generally at their best the day they are laid. Some man-made materials can deteriorate rapidly, particularly with respect to colour, staining and breakage.

The historic character of Elgin town centre was restored by the careful choice of natural materials and has provided a finish that is durable, resistant to heavy goods service vehicles, attractive and appropriate in terms of colour and texture. The phased approach to implementation prevented this quality being compromised despite strict budgetary constraints.

Kilmarnock, Granite setts

Coventry, Man-made materials

St Giles Church, Elgin High Street

John Dickie Street, Kilmarnock

In Conwy, a unique historic town with multiple pressures in a constrained historic setting, pedestrian priority measures achieved a balance between conservation and enhancement of the environment. A range of pedestrian priority and conservation projects have been implemented over the last ten years which have significantly enhanced the attractions of the town centre.

A long term approach to enhancement has been adopted in Kilmarnock. The measures implemented have not compromised on quality, durability or coverage. The extended lifespan, perhaps over 100 years, of the scheme should off-set the initial high capital cost. The use of natural materials has produced an attractive streetscape and has enhanced civic pride and business confidence.

Planned and careful maintenance and cleaning are required to enhance the lifespan of a scheme. The quality of design and workmanship is also essential in ensuring longevity of schemes.

CHAPTER 3
Resolving Conflict:
The Pedestrianisation Debate

The Evolution of Pedestrianisation

Full and partial pedestrianisation as improvements to urban spaces in town centres has been wide spread. Understanding the pedestrianisation debate is central to successful urban spaces in town centres. Colin Buchanan (1961) suggested that pedestrians should have the freedom of the city and should be free to; wander, sit, look, meet, gossip, contemplate the scenery and the architecture and the history. He also suggested that they should be treated with dignity, and that discipline is the last thing they need.

The first wave of pedestrianisation in Great Britain occurred in the 1970s implementing the town plans of the 1960s. Many schemes, particularly in London (Pimlico and Barnsbury) followed the approach advocated in 'Traffic in Towns' (1963) and developed environmental areas, which linked traffic restraint with housing improvements.

The need for pedestrianisation schemes was not well analysed or documented at the time. The overriding requirement was to try to balance the needs of the pedestrian and the car user. Hence many of the early schemes were engineering led, paying little regard to aesthetic quality or human behaviour.

In 1981, approximately 1,450 pedestrianised precincts existed in towns and cities in the UK and most were favourably received at the time (Roberts, 1981). By 1995 approximately 37% of the prime shopping streets in the UK were pedestrianised compared with less than 5% in 1971 (Colliers Erdman Lewis, 1995). However, many pedestrianised areas are now dated and require a radical rethink. There is still much of the urban environment which is unsuitable for pedestrians, especially in town and city centres.

Faced with increasing out-of-town competition there has been a considerable level of pedestrianisation within town centres in recent years, either new or extended pedestrianised areas. Recent research (Colliers Erdman Lewis, 1995) has cast doubt on the wider application of pedestrianisation. The elimination of traffic from unsuccessful public places is not always the most suitable solution (Falk, 1995). Many pedestrianisation schemes have failed to revitalise declining town centres. This situation is particularly evident within the USA where there are many examples of failed pedestrianised streets which have been re-opened to traffic to make them safer.

PEDESTRIANISATION: THE COMMERCIAL PERSPECTIVE

Recent evidence suggests that shop rents in prime pedestrianised streets are no higher than in prime vehicular streets and both continue to under perform rental growth in shopping centres (Colliers Erdman Lewis, 1995). The case for pedestrianised streets improving rental performance remains to be proved. Pedestrianisation should be considered as one of a package of measures which may help to regenerate a town centre. As mentioned earlier, the problems of using pedestrianisation

Derby's pedestrianisation scheme

as a universal cure-all in town centres can be observed in the USA where 'dead zones' or no-go areas are common in Central Business District cores.

Surprisingly, very few local authorities have attempted to monitor the impact of pedestrianisation schemes, other than undertaking traffic flow counts. Monitoring changes in pedestrian flow after pedestrianisation schemes have been implemented is rarely undertaken. However, Lincolnshire County Council did undertake 'before' and 'after' surveys for seven pedestrianisation schemes, which demonstrated that the majority of affected businesses were positive about the scheme. However, one scheme did appear to be 'unsuccessful' with a majority indicating that the scheme had been harmful rather than beneficial, reducing trading performance.

Generally multiple traders within Lincolnshire were more in favour of pedestrianisation than independent traders. Clothing and household goods retailers were generally more positive than food and convenience retailers. This division in retailers' attitudes is also evident from business surveys undertaken within the case study towns and the views expressed by high street retailers.

Environ (1992) summarises evidence from pedestrianisation impact appraisals in 19 towns in Europe and North America. Their research concluded that the vast majority of pedestrianisation schemes have had a positive influence on trade. However, evidence shows that construction work can cause trade to fall in the short term. This disruption has been evident in some of the case study towns.

In general the 19 projects reviewed had improved trade for the majority of traders following implementation. Increases of up to 40% in turnover were claimed by some traders. There was also a shift in attitudes amongst traders during the development process. In many cases traders were reluctant initially, although most were positive after implementation. For example, extensive pedestrianisation within Derby city centre has been both commercially and functionally successful. Early indications suggest that pedestrian flowcounts have improved by over 15% since the scheme was implemented.

Derby has also attracted an impressive list of new retailers since the scheme was completed including Virgin Records, Disney, Oasis and Waterstones. Major refurbishments by existing retailers have also been completed including; BHS, Littlewoods, Boots and Marks & Spencer. Interest in potential development sites and refurbishment grants within the City Centre have also re-emerged.

Before and after pedestrian counts in Darlington – following the pedestrianisation of Skinnergate and the surrounding areas showed a 14% increase after pedestrianisation. Research also indicated a high level of public support for the scheme (87%). Approximately 90% of the public believed that pedestrianisation had made the area a more pleasant shopping environment. The scheme was also popular with the majority of businesses affected by the scheme.

An appraisal of pedestrianisation schemes by the Highlands Regional Council collated trading performance data for five towns in Scotland. This research suggested that trade had improved after pedestrianisation in three towns and had remained the same in the other two towns. In one town an increase in trade was recorded by retailers in the core pedestrianised area, but trade had not improved in untouched secondary areas. In general the majority of traders were positive about pedestrianisation schemes. Public satisfaction was even greater.

Clearly, some retailers oppose pedestrianisation as a concept. They perceive pedestrianisation as detrimental to their trade, particularly those who rely heavily on passing trade. Pavement widening and other traffic restrictions are seen as more suitable alternatives by some traders. This message emerged in the analysis of pedestrianisation schemes within the case study towns.

Convenient car and public transport access are viewed as critical by many retailers. Therefore, pedestrianisation schemes that restrict access can be seen to be harmful. Conversely, many comparison goods retailers perceive pedestrianisation and traffic restrictions as desirable and beneficial to trade and amenity.

Business surveys indicate that the main operational problems arising from pedestrianisation and other enhancement schemes relate to delivery access. The loss of car parking spaces, particularly for people with disabilities, is also a major concern. Restricted access and the loss of car parking or bus stops can be detrimental to some operators, particularly traders who rely on passing trade such as newsagents, off-licenses, takeaways or convenience stores. Retailers who sell bulky items such as furniture also benefit from nearby on-street parking.

The provision of easily identifiable car parking with well signposted car park routes can enhance turnover for these types of traders. In general, pedestrianisation will make servicing more difficult, particularly in high streets with poor rear access.

There is no recipe for success except a careful evaluation of uses and requirements of individual town centres. Vehicle restricted areas will work in some towns and not in others. What works will depend on how the scheme is received: consultation and partnership approaches will facilitate success.

KEY REQUIREMENTS FOR SUCCESSFUL PEDESTRIANISATION SCHEMES

The key requirement in appraising the value of pedestrianisation is to understand the needs and aspirations of the users, occupiers and investors in the town centre. Beyond this, schemes must embrace the wider objectives for the town centre and the budget that is available.

Pedestrian priority is essential if the right balance between traffic and people is to be achieved. This means that all pedestrian activities across the whole town centre must be understood and prioritised. From the moment the visitor or consumer leaves the car, cycle, bus or train they are starting to evaluate the town centre as a pedestrian. Routes to and from the main attractions should be safe, attractive and well signposted. Car parks, bus and train stations should be user friendly, safe and graffiti free. Throughout the town centre, the relationship between pedestrians and traffic needs to be evaluated.

Advice in PPG6 'Town Centres and Retail Developments' (June 1996) on monitoring change and measuring vitality and viability in town centres will help to resolve the difficult question of balance between pedestrian and vehicle priority. In particular, indicators such as pedestrian flows, measures of accessibility, environmental quality and customer views and behaviour will be important. After all, traffic engineers calculate precise figures for vehicle flows but the interface with the pedestrian is still not measured or well understood.

The impact of pedestrianisation on the image of the town centres during the night is also an important consideration. Towns with a lively evening economy may keep their pedestrianised areas busy and safe, whilst other less vibrant towns may become deserted attracting gangs of youths and giving an unsafe image.

The extent or coverage of pedestrianisation also needs careful consideration. Extensive areas of pedestrianisation often works best in large metropolitan cities, with inner ring roads which allow the exclusion of traffic from the centre. These centres also benefit from a mix of uses which generate significant numbers of visitors (during the day and night). The decision to implement pedestrianisation and the total exclusion of traffic must not be taken lightly. Alternative options, such as pavement widening, restricted access for certain vehicles and traffic calming should be explored.

CHAPTER 4
Measuring Success

Why Measure Success?

Despite the significant level of investment on improving urban spaces within town centres, little effort has been made to identify or measure success. As indicated in the previous sections within this guide, successful urban spaces can be considered from a number of different perspectives. However, to date little research has been undertaken to quantify the level of impact that well planned and managed urban spaces have had on the vitality and viability of town centres.

Our survey of local authorities indicated that the 285 responding authorities had implemented major urban space enhancement schemes in 438 towns across the country, since 1985. The majority of schemes identified (73%) were considered to be successful by the local authority. However, only 28% of authorities had undertaken any form of evaluation or measurement of the success of their schemes.

Little evidence has been collected to quantify the value-for-money or importance of well planned and maintained urban spaces despite the high level of investment in recent years. Clearly, this lack of evidence has not helped to convince retailers and investors that improvements to urban spaces is money well spent. Many retailers and investors will remain sceptical if evaluation and monitoring of schemes is not improved.

In addition, PPG6 (Revised June 1996) urges local authorities to monitor the performance of their town centres in general. Clearly, this recommended monitoring should also examine the impact that urban space improvements have had on the overall vitality and viability of the town centre.

INDICATORS OF SUCCESS

PPG6 provides guidance on measuring vitality and viability of town centres and lists a number of indicators, as described below.

- *Diversity of uses:* how much space is in use for different functions. The diversity of uses within a town centre can be compared with other towns using Goad Plan data.

- *Retailer representation and future intentions:* demand from retailers wanting to come into the town, or to change their representation in the town. Future intentions can be established by canvassing operators.

- *Shopping rents:* pattern of movement in Zone A rents within the primary shopping areas. Zone A rents are the primary measure for standardising and comparing rental levels and identifying changes over time. They generally relate to the rent payable on the first 20 foot depth of the shop unit and can be used to compare rental levels for shop units of varying size.

- *Proportion of vacant street level property:* vacancy rates can be monitored over time or compared with the national situation using data from Goad Plans.

- *Commercial yields on non-domestic properties:* Yields can be used to measure changes in investment confidence, and are set by the market based on experience and comparisons. The yield is the income (rent) from a property as a percentage of the capital value. Generally, lower yields reflect greater investor confidence about future growth in the value of their investment.

- *Pedestrian flows:* the numbers and movement of people on the streets. A programme of pedestrian flowcounts can be used to monitor the performance of specific parts of the town centre or the centre as a whole.

- *Accessibility:* the ease and convenience of access by different means of travel. The availability of convenient and ample car parking, bus stops and pedestrian routes are all important considerations in determining accessibility.

- *Customer views and behaviour:* monitored by regular surveys.

- *Perception of safety and occurrence of crime.*

- *Environmental quality of the town centre:* such as pollution, noise, clutter, litter and graffiti.

The PPG6 list of indicators of vitality and viability provides a valuable guide to the overall performance of a town centre, particularly when time series data is available. The impact of urban space improvement schemes may influence many of these factors. Therefore, the success of a scheme may be quantified by analysing the measures of vitality and viability listed within PPG6. For example, information can be collected before and after a scheme is implemented in order to assess the level of success.

Many of the PPG6 indicators can be measured easily. Time series data can be obtained from published sources of information or collated from empirical research. For example; pedestrian flow, rental levels, yields, reported crimes, accidents, retailers requirements, vacancies and the range of facilities available. These indicators are all quantifiable, whilst other measurements of success are more subjective, such as the quality of the environment.

Unfortunately, information on the trading performance of town centres is generally unavailable. Understandably, retailers are wary about disclosing confidential financial information. However, business or operator surveys can examine trends and opinions on trading performance, without disclosing precise monetary values.

ESTABLISHING A BASELINE

Clearly, many extraneous factors will influence these measures within town or city centres. For example, national and regional economic trends, out-of-town retail developments, or improvements within nearby competing centres. Excellent design and management of urban spaces cannot fully offset other constraints or weaknesses of the town centre as a whole. The quality of the town centre compared to the competition is of significant importance.

Before the benefits of a scheme can be assessed it is necessary to establish an appropriate baseline. Maintaining the status quo within a town centre may in itself be an achievement, due to a decline in the local economy in general or the effects of major out-of-town retail developments. The recession and out-of-town retail development has clearly had an impact on many town centres, reflected by national information on shop vacancy levels, Zone A rents, pedestrian flows and commercial yields.

Published evidence suggests that average pedestrian flowcounts in town centres across Great Britain fell by 6.6% during the recession (Source: Pedestrian Market Research Services 1987 to 1994). Furthermore, shop vacancy levels within town centres increased significantly across the country due to the effects of the recession and the over-provision of new retail floorspace during the property boom in the late 1980s. Unit vacancy levels in Great Britain increased from 8% to nearly 14% between 1987-1995 (Source: Chas E Goad).

The effects of the recession were clearly mirrored by increases in retail yields. Average yields in Great Britain increased by 38% between 1988 and 1992 (Source: Investment Property Database), indicating reduced confidence in the market, but have recovered since 1992. National trends in Zone A rental levels have also been affected by the recession. Prime pitch Zone A rents increased by approximately 80% between 1985 and 1990, but have fallen during the recession.

Clearly, any evaluation of urban space enhancement schemes implemented in recent years must be considered against this national context. It is also important to note that there are many reasons why shops become vacant. Trading difficulties and reduced numbers of shoppers are not always the cause.

OTHER NON-COMMERCIAL MEASURES OF SUCCESS

There are many other environmental benefits of well planned and managed urban spaces that can also be measured. For example, projects can have a positive benefit on road safety, noise and pollution. The Department of Transport's Bypass Demonstration Project provides a comprehensive analysis of the success of urban space schemes, including pedestrianisation and traffic calming measures. This study indicated that average speeds within six case study towns were reduced by up to 50% in some streets as a result of the measures implemented.

The measures implemented also had a major impact on the perception of safety amongst the general public and businesses. Recorded accidents reduced significantly in most of the case study towns. In some cases no accidents had been recorded since implementation. However, these types of schemes can create new problem areas, particularly around the edges of the pedestrianised area. Clear definition and separation of areas for both pedestrians and vehicles, along with traffic calming measures have prevented the creation of new accident black spots.

A 20 mph speed limit zone implemented in Market Harborough town centre along with imaginatively designed traffic calming features have reduced traffic speeds and improved safety in and around the town centre. Noise and nitrogen dioxide concentration levels also reduced significantly.

Careful junction design in Petersfield has modified drivers' behaviour, reducing speeds whilst maintaining accessibility. The scheme has used cleverly tactile materials to avoid the excessive use of road markings, bollards, chicanes and ramps. Before and after surveys showed marked reductions in noise and nitrogen dioxide concentrations (over 40%).

Traffic calming measures and regular pedestrian crossing points in Stowmarket have been provided to improve safety. The pedestrian areas have been clearly defined using light coloured slabs. The carriageway and lay-bys have been laid with darker brick pavers. No recorded serious accidents have occurred since the scheme was implemented compared with the annual average of 3-4 accidents before the scheme.

RAISING STANDARDS

Well designed and managed urban spaces have an important role in raising the overall design quality within a town centre. Improved urban spaces can help to raise standards and act as a valuable benchmark against which new developments or proposals can be judged. Standard raising can improve a local authority's powers to control the design and quality of new developments.

The positive impact on civic pride can also be significant. Improvements can affect the way our town centres are perceived and treated, reducing the level of litter and vandalism.

CHAPTER 5
Commercial Success:
The Evidence

Well planned and managed improvements to urban spaces are usually welcomed by the general public. The benefits to businesses are less clear. The benefits are wide ranging, but many indicators of success are difficult to quantify. Analysis of urban space enhancement schemes does not always present a clear picture. Commercial impact can vary significantly from scheme to scheme. Variations in success between individual businesses or specific areas within the same town can also be considerable. However, the case study schemes and other research demonstrate that the results from business surveys and other measures of success are generally positive.

TRADING PERFORMANCE

A recent survey commissioned by Boots the Chemist and undertaken by Urban Management Initiatives looked at the takings of a sample of high street stores between 1990-1995. This survey provided firm evidence that well promoted and managed town centres, including towns where environmental and streetscape improvements had been undertaken, are likely to perform better than poorly managed and maintained town centres. The research also highlighted the major impact that other factors, such as parking, access and out-of-town shopping developments, can have on trading performance.

As discussed in Section 3, evidence regarding the impact of pedestrianisation on trading performance is mixed. However, it is clear from available research that pedestrianisation and other environmental improvements can, in the right circumstances have a positive impact on trading performance, but the benefits do vary from business to business. The impact on trading performance can be particularly significant in run down areas which have been regenerated.

Survey evidence summarised by Environ (1992) suggests that turnover increases of up to 40% can be achieved. Urban space enhancements and the creation of a new cafe quarter in Mill Lane, Cardiff increased restaurant trade by between 120-500%. However, evidence from other towns suggests that the impact on trading performance is usually less dramatic (up to 15%) and the full benefits can take a few years to be realised. However, it is important to note that the marginal increase in turnover achieved in many towns has been sufficient to offset the overall cost of the urban space enhancement schemes implemented.

Mill Lane, Cardiff, a commercial success

For example, the recent enhancement of the pedestrianised precincts in Coventry has had a positive impact on trading levels within the city centre. Retailers have reported increased trade and customers from a wider area, with shops out performing branches in surrounding towns. These reports are supported by increases in footfall counts (up 3.5% on week days and up 25% on Saturdays) and in short stay car park usage (up 30% since 1990). However, evidence in Coventry does suggest that the disruption during the implementation of the improvements was detrimental to trading levels.

The implementation of pedestrianisation and urban space enhancement within Solihull High Street has also shown early signs of commercial success, with a 10% increase in the use of town centre car parks.

BUSINESS PERCEPTIONS

Urban space enhancement schemes can be contentious amongst affected businesses, primarily due to the disruption caused and alterations to parking and servicing. However, well planned improvements can be popular with both businesses and the public, particularly where there has been a strong partnership approach during the planning and implementation of the scheme.

Business surveys conducted in four of the case study towns (Darlington, Hemel Hempstead, Kilmarnock and Windsor) indicate that there was generally a high level of satisfaction (65-90%) amongst traders following the implementation of urban space improvements. Involvement throughout the implementation process was the key to this high level of satisfaction.

Avoiding Disruption

The implementation of paving and other town centre environmental works can in some circumstances have a detrimental impact on pedestrian flows and trading performances, making the scheme very unpopular with businesses. Disruption during implementation works can be severe. Many implementing authorities have been criticised for their lack of commercial sense with regard to the timing of implementation.

In general, it is desirable to implement proposals in the shortest period possible. However, in many cases a short implementation period is not feasible due to physical or funding constraints, and a phased approach needs to be adopted. A phased approach does provide an opportunity to test schemes which include radical changes. Programming of works should where possible avoid peak seasons, such as the Christmas period, or the summer peak for tourist resorts or historic towns. A staged, phased implementation programme can be adopted to avoid peak trading periods.

PROPERTY PERSPECTIVE

The benefits of urban space enhancement schemes for property investors are interrelated with the benefits for occupiers and users. Improvements in the number of shoppers, trade, and the environmental quality of a town centre can increase investment confidence. Important measures of success for an investor are recognised by PPG6 as vacancy levels, rental growth and commercial yields.

Evidence from the case study towns suggests that urban space enhancement is unlikely to have a dramatic impact on vacancy levels, yields or rental growth, except in very rundown secondary shopping areas. These measures need to be implemented in conjunction with other improvements in order to uplift significantly the retail property market within a town centre. Furthermore, the impact of urban space enhancement schemes on these measures take time to be realised. Measuring these long term improvements cannot be precise, given that there are a large number of other determining factors, as discussed in Section 4.

As indicated in Section 3, research undertaken by Colliers Erdman Lewis (1995) suggested that pedestrianisation schemes have had no detectable impact on rental levels over a three year period after schemes had been completed. On average, prime pedestrianised and non-pedestrianised streets had performed similarly in terms of rental. Closer examination of the rental performances showed that disruption during implementation had had a negative impact on rental levels during the first year, but rental growth had returned to the national trend in the second and third year. It is also important to note that the rental growth experienced after pedestrianisation varied significantly from centre to centre (−10% to +8%), suggesting that some schemes were more successful than others and/or other factors had influenced rental changes.

The evaluation of our case study towns also suggests that rental growth varies considerably from town to town. Several towns have performed well during the recession compared with neighbouring towns. However in general, yields rents and vacancy levels information for the case study towns indicates that few urban enhancement schemes have had a significant impact on these property measures. The impact of environmental improvements has been most evident in secondary shopping areas, or areas that were run down, rather than prime shopping streets.

In general, urban space improvements do not appear to have had a major impact on vacancy rates, as demonstrated by the case study towns, although vacancy levels have dropped in many towns where urban space improvements have been implemented, despite the national upward trend. The most dramatic impact on vacancy levels was experienced in enhancement schemes which targeted rundown shopping areas, which had a high level of vacancies before implementation.

Private Sector Investment

The impact of urban space enhancement schemes on the main property measures provides a mixed picture. However, the positive impact on private sector investment is more evident. Many of the case study schemes have acted as major catalysts to private sector investment within the town centre.

Urban space improvements can have indirect benefits, by raising the quality of the environment and improving civic pride significantly within a town centre. The implementation of a scheme can also help to stimulate investment activities including:

- major town centre developments;

- renovation and redevelopments;

- redecoration or renewal of shop frontages; and

- major shop re-fits.

For example, the development of the town relief road and pedestrianisation in Ilford has helped to reverse decline experienced during the 1970s. The scheme acted as a catalyst to secure £125 million of private sector investment, including the development of a major new covered shopping centre. This inward investment greatly exceeded the cost of the relief road and urban space improvements (by a factor of four).

Pedestrianisation and other improvements in Solihull have helped to encourage a number of major operators in the town to either extend or reinvest in their stores, including Marks and Spencer, WH Smith, Beatties and BHS. Proposals for the £90 million development of a 300,000 sq. ft shopping mall have also progressed since the scheme was implemented.

The package of urban space improvements implemented in Coventry acted as an important catalyst for major private sector investment in the form of new shopping centres at West Orchard and Cathedral Lanes and voids within the precinct areas have declined in recent years. Overall vacancy levels are now very low.

Mill Lane, Cardiff

The creation and enhancement of public spaces can be linked successfully with wider regeneration and development initiatives. A joint public and private sector initiative was established in Aberdeen to address the declining physical fabric within the city centre. The proposals implemented have had broad ranging benefits, and have generated significant private sector leverage. The City Centre Project has implemented a large number of regeneration schemes, which have provided over 1,500 new homes within the city centre. Urban space enhancements have been cross funded by residential schemes and the redevelopment of derelict buildings to provide new shop units.

The new *Cafe Quarter* at Mill Lane in Cardiff demonstrates how a run down secondary area can be transformed by urban space enhancement and careful theming. Direct investment as a result of the Mill Lane initiative has been estimated at around £4.5 million, from an £800,000 investment by the public sector. This spin-off investment included: new occupiers, refurbishment of premises and the adjacent Wyndham Arcade. The number of vacant units has also fallen. An estimated additional 70 part-time jobs have been created during the summer months.

REDUCING CRIME

In 1994/95 crime cost retailers £1.5 billion (British Retail Consortium) – approximately 1% of total turnover. Retailers invest over £500 million on crime prevention, including security staff, cash collection and surveillance equipment, each year. High levels of crime in a specific area can lead to shop closures and can deter new retailers. Crime is a major issue for all traders and influences investment decisions. The public's perception of crime can also be important in choosing a town centre to shop.

Careful use of street furniture and good lighting can hinder ram-raiders and deter criminals. It can also make the public feel safer. Good design and active management measures such as close circuit television (CCTV) have proved to be most successful. There is strong empirical evidence that well managed urban spaces with CCTV and radio link schemes significantly reduce crime, including theft, attacks and vandalism.

For example, crime in Folkestone fell by almost a third in the first three months after CCTV was introduced. Car related thefts reduced by 50%. A radio security system in Wolverhampton reduced shoplifting by 38% during its first year. However, systems need to be well planned, comprehensive and suitably staffed to prevent crime from moving to un-monitored areas.

The city centre of Coventry has become one of the safest areas in the city. All forms of crime levels have fallen dramatically (30-40% reduction since 1990). CCTV in conjunction with Retail Radio Link and an Alcohol Free Zone have been instrumental in reducing vandalism and theft. The installation of clear signage and removal of pavement obstacles have served to enhance shoppers' perceptions of safety.

URBAN SPACE IMPROVEMENTS – VALUE FOR MONEY?

The cost of major town centre urban space enhancement schemes including pedestrianisation typically range between £1 million to £10 million, largely dependent on the quality of the materials used and the extent or coverage of the scheme. In most cases the cost of urban space schemes will constitute less than 2% of the total annual turnover of retail businesses within the town centre. Therefore, modest improvements in trading performance will be sufficient to offset the cost of most schemes, without taking into account other benefits such as reduced crime and accidents, and private sector investment.

There is sufficient empirical evidence to demonstrate that well planned, implemented and maintained urban space improvements can have a positive impact on the trading performance of most town centre occupiers, although the full effect of the scheme may take 2-3 years to be realised. The most successful schemes are usually only one element of a wider action orientated strategy for the town centre as a whole. Therefore, urban design or traffic management measures should never be considered in isolation, but should be linked to broader long term objectives and proposals for the town centre.

There is strong empirical evidence to suggest that urban space schemes, which are part of a wider package of proposals, can have a measurable impact on trading performance. Analysis of pedestrian flowcounts, business surveys or car park usage data indicates that trading performance can, typically, be improved by up to 15%, although greater increases can be achieved within targeted secondary or run down areas.

The cost of projects can generate further financial benefits, including:

- indirect private sector investment;

- reductions in the number of accidents (emergency service costs); and

- reductions in crime (theft from businesses and the public).

The indirect impact of environmental works on property investment patterns can be substantial. In some cases indirect inward investment has exceeded scheme costs by a factor of four. Taking into account the range of other potential financial benefits, the 'multiplier' effect achieved from well planned urban space enhancement schemes could be even greater, up to a factor of ten.

CHAPTER 6
Approach to Implementation

Planning and Management Process

Many local authorities may appear to have rushed into urban space enhancement schemes without examining fully all the relevant issues and the interrelationships between urban spaces and other key functions of their town or city centre. Often local authorities have had to respond very quickly in order to utilise available resources or to bid for limited funding. Therefore, it has not always been possible to undertake a comprehensive evaluation and planning process. As a result, many implementing bodies have had to learn from their mistakes.

The first wave of urban space enhancement schemes during the 1960s and 1970s were in many cases engineering led, concentrating on the functional requirements of vehicles. As a result, the aesthetic quality of schemes and the requirements of the pedestrian were neglected. The aesthetic quality of more recent schemes has improved generally. However, the shift towards better design has in some cases been at the expense of the functional and practical requirements which have not been given full consideration. Clearly, there is a need for a balanced approach incorporating the expertise of a range of disciplines, including engineers, architects, urban and landscape designers and planners.

GOOD PRACTICE FRAMEWORK

There are a number of approaches which can be followed to achieve a good quality streetscape. However, as the appearance of the street is still the responsibility of the local authority, a process which is publicly recognisable and understood is usually required.

Figure 1 sets out a broad framework for the planning and management process for urban space enhancement within town centres. The assessment of case study towns has demonstrated that urban space enhancement schemes which have evolved from a clearly staged process are generally more successful, particularly in terms of business and shopper satisfaction.

This process assumes that the local authority is the principal initiator for improving the streetscape. However, as with many town centre projects, a series of partnerships will need to be established with investors, occupiers and users to ensure joint 'ownership' of the proposals. A town centre manager may be the best person to co-ordinate these activities.

The process highlighted in Figure 1 attempts to link the planning, design and management of urban spaces with other relevant town centre considerations, including transport, planning, tourism, development proposals and the aspirations of businesses and the general public. However, this indicative process is not rigid, and is designed to provide strategic guidance only. It demonstrates a potential route that implementing bodies may choose to follow. The process is also ongoing and iterative, which allows implementing authorities to respond quickly and effectively to opportunities as they arise, limiting mistakes and improving success. The framework can also be incorporated into the normal development plan process and town centre management and maintenance initiatives.

Figure 1 – Planning and Management Process

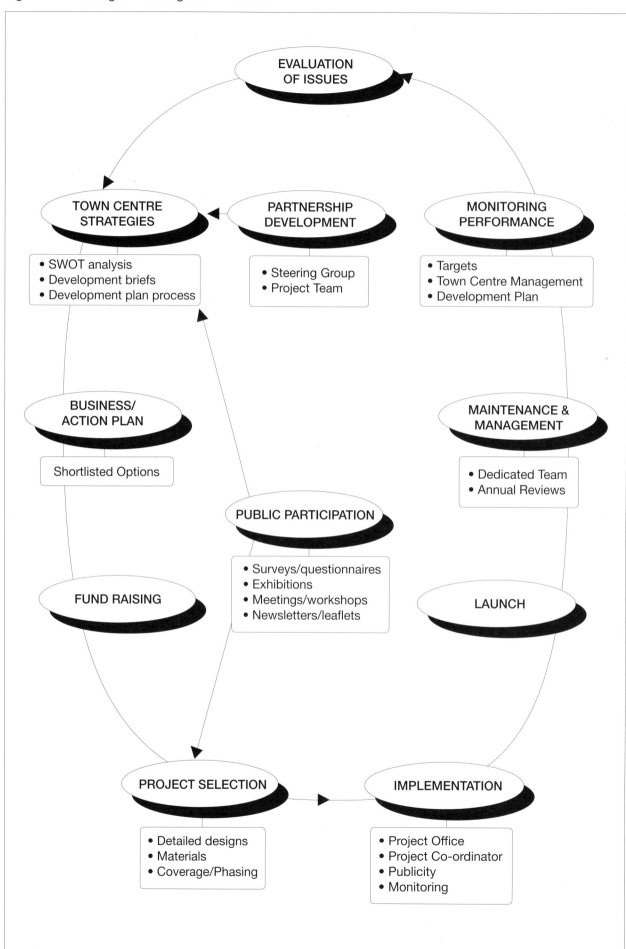

EVALUATION OF ISSUES

Emerging proposals for the regeneration of town or city centres should be underpinned by an evaluation of the key issues relating to the vitality and viability of that centre. Ongoing monitoring of changes in the performance of the centre, as advocated by the revised PPG6, should provide the appropriate context for this evaluation. The evaluation should identify major problems faced by the centre, including competing centres and out-of-town retail development. It should identify and explore the key roles of the centre and determine the interrelationship between complementary and competing functions. It may be appropriate at this stage to undertake survey analysis to determine the role and catchment area of the centre and to establish resident and business perceptions. This stage should also include:

● a physical audit of the streetscape – the results can be tabled as a SWOT analysis which will highlight historic features and other contextual assets, as well as eyesores and problem areas; and

● a user survey or workshop groups – an ethnographic approach may be the most appropriate particularly for interest groups such as the disabled. Mental maps of the town centre have been found to be very illuminating: illustrating users' perceptions of the strengths and weaknesses of the town centre environment. Visitor surveys can also be appropriate if a wider audience is important and a higher response rate required.

This evaluation may be part of the wider analysis undertaken during the development plan preparation process, and should form a suitable context for the preparation of specific objectives for the centre.

TOWN CENTRE STRATEGIES AND PARTNERSHIP DEVELOPMENT

A clear town centre strategy needs to be developed which will focus on a wide range of issues. The physical fabric of building frontages and the user quality of the street environment should be an important element within this strategy. The results and information collated during the evaluation stage should form an appropriate basis for this strategy.

SWOT Analysis

The evaluation process should provide a basis for an analysis of the centre's strengths and weaknesses and the identification of opportunities and threats (a SWOT analysis). The SWOT analysis should explore a range of topic areas, which could include shopping, employment, tourism, car parking, public transport access, car access, the evening economy, conservation and environmental design. Clearly urban spaces are an important part of this analysis, and have strong linkages with all topic areas. Therefore, any improvements to urban spaces or management measures must be based on a clear understanding of a broad range of issues, not only urban design or engineering considerations.

The findings of the analysis should be transformed into realisable recommendations for improving the town centre. These recommendations should be pulled together into a comprehensive long term strategy for the centre, or a series of interrelated strategies addressing separate topic areas.

Development Plan Process and Development Briefs

The preparation of the strategy should ideally be linked to the development plan preparation process. The parameters for emerging development opportunities can be quantified through the preparation of development briefs for key sites/areas. The strategy will need to include feasibility appraisals of potential improvements, including urban space enhancement schemes and pedestrianisation.

Partnership Development

The strategy preparation process is a suitable stage at which to build partnerships between local authorities, local traders, user groups, business organisations, landowners and other interest groups. Investors, occupiers and users of the town centre will all need to be persuaded of the approach.

Agreement and broad ownership of the conceptual strategy and vision at this early stage is essential to the future success of selected improvements. The role of the town centre manager is vital, bridging the gap between the local authority and the private sector.

For the effective enhancement of a centre the project should follow a fully co-ordinated approach. A partnership process provides an impetus for setting and achieving an overall design strategy. Joint working with Planning and Highways Departments ensures that implementation of the enhancement scheme minimises disturbance as far as possible, whilst achieving its overall defined objectives.

The scale of the project may require that other bodies are consulted during all stages of the work. The relevant public bodies should receive full notification. It is far more effective to consult at an early stage. A good working relationship, preferably through the town centre manager, with those who may be affected by the scheme is essential if the scheme is to be implemented as smoothly as possible.

Steering Group and Project Team

During the preparation of the agreed town centre strategy it may be desirable to establish a *steering group and project team(s)* to oversee and manage subsequent stages within the process and the implementation of the plan. The steering group can be drawn from town centre partnership structures and would be responsible for overall guidance during implementation. The steering group may consist of council members and officers, the town centre manager, and representatives from local trader organisations, conservation groups, public interest groups, the police and other services.

Specific *project teams* should also be formed responsible for the day-to-day co-ordination of projects. These teams should be a multi-disciplinary (council officers and consultants), perhaps with other representatives from the *steering group*. The teams would usually need to meet regularly, reporting back to the steering group as appropriate. The steering group and project teams, with the support of the town centre manager, should ultimately take on the responsibility or retain some active involvement in the ongoing management and maintenance of the centre.

Examples of Good Practice

Derby

The Derby City Centre Management Team, a partnership between the public sector and key city centre businesses, led to the successful implementation of a wide range of pedestrianisation and other urban space improvements. The partnership has built on the success of these improvements to strengthen the overall vitality and viability of the city centre. A number of management and promotional initiatives have helped to make Derby more competitive.

Coventry

Urban space enhancement proposals implemented in Coventry were part of a broader strategy for the city centre. The City Council used the private sector's development and management expertise to construct a comprehensive action orientated regeneration strategy. The regeneration strategy has undoubtedly transformed the quality of the environment and public spaces, introducing new activities and events. The image of Coventry and the level of civic pride have improved significantly.

Revitalised Precinct, Coventry

CrownGate. Worcester

Worcester

The CrownGate redevelopment in Worcester exemplifies a fully co-ordinated approach to city centre planning that has ensured the City's future viability. Public spaces and permeability throughout the city centre were improved. The genuine partnership approach between the public and private sector broadened expectations and resulted in a scheme that achieved far more than was initially envisaged.

BUSINESS OR ACTION PLAN

The recommendations and objectives contained within the centre strategy need to be translated into a business or action plan. The plan should translate the concepts into precise projects with time scales attached. The plan should contain a broad range of co-ordinated proposals for the enhancement, management and promotion of the centre as a whole. Improvements to urban spaces and pedestrianisation schemes may be one element of this overall package of measures. The plan should focus on:

- priorities and timetables;
- manpower resources;
- funding sources;
- capital and revenue budgets; and
- specific projects proposals with a shortlist of options.

The business/action plan should identify specific projects and should provide a short list of options.

FUND RAISING

The selection and implementation of projects identified in the business/action plans will be dependent on the level of funds available. Partnership development and the preparation of suitable strategies should have a positive benefit on subsequent fund raising exercises. The promotional and persuasive skills of the town centre manager will also be vital during this stage. The production of a detailed town centre strategy and business/action plan should provide a sound basis for preparing convincing bids for funding.

PROJECT SELECTION

The key to the success of a scheme must be careful project planning and selection. In order to achieve the desired output the plan must incorporate analysis of the cash flow needed for the scheme, timescale of the scheme, impact on the surrounding area, for example road closures, necessary consultation and any consents required. Careful and considered planning should minimise the disturbances during the construction phase and the project work phase ultimately maximising the positive benefits of the scheme.

Having identified the preferred project with shortlisted options within the action plan detailed designs can be prepared. However, before final detailed designs are prepared, further survey and appraisal work needs to be undertaken to consider the:

- functional and aesthetic requirements;
- findings of a detailed site survey;
- the suitability, durability and cost of different materials;
- the appropriate coverage of the scheme;
- phasing requirements;
- an assessment of ongoing maintenance and management issues;

- co-ordination between cleaning and design regimes;

- funding constraints; and

- constraints on construction.

Detailed Designs

Perhaps the most vital element of the scheme is the actual design. It is designers who will need to put the technical awareness into practice, without forgetting the practicalities involved in actually designing an urban streetscape. Vision is a vital element but the scheme must be in keeping with the characteristics of the town and also the characteristics of those people who regularly use the facilities. The design does not always have to be innovative but it must feel comfortable to the users.

Increasingly, competitive tendering is used in selecting a design team. It is crucial in analysing the various merits of the design schemes to look at the quality of each scheme and the cost implications. For comparative analysis the desired quality of the scheme should be clearly established from the outset and all options or tenders should be judged against these quality criteria.

Materials, Coverage and Phasing

The level of funding for the project must ensure that the desired quality of work is achievable. Uncertainty regarding timing of the scheme and/or changes in material costs will impact on delivered quality unless the scheme incorporates flexibility in input costs.

Ultimately, if the predetermined quality cannot be procured, attention must focus on adapting the finances of the scheme. This can be achieved through delaying payment by phasing the scheme, or more obviously by reducing the physical extent of the scheme. The latter however may impact upon the desired improvement. Depending on the scheme, the quality may be lowered without rendering the scheme ineffective.

The design team must be fully aware of any constraints in terms of quality of materials and selection of materials to be used. Any constraints should therefore be established early on. The whole lifecycle costing must take into account the appearance of materials over time, the performance delivery, public utility requirements, future disruption and any capital maintenance costs.

Example of Good Practice
Bournemouth

Budgetary constraints postponed the implementation of Bournemouth Borough Council's plans to close a major roundabout within the town centre to create a new town square. However, the council recognised that alternative measures were required to alleviate constraints to pedestrian movement across the town centre. The low cost interim solution implemented has created an effective and attractive pedestrian route and a popular public space. The council has also retained the option of implementing the full scheme, if funding becomes available in the future. The scheme demonstrates that temporary or partial solutions can be successful and significantly more desirable than the 'do nothing' scenario, particularly when one is faced with severe conflict problems between pedestrians and vehicles.

PUBLIC PARTICIPATION

The preparation of the town centre strategy and business/action plan for the centre can provide a forward looking framework for involving the wider general public. The public participation process can go beyond consultation with recognised interest groups, and should instil a strong feeling of public ownership and real involvement. The participation exercise should focus on the broad shortlisted options highlighted in the action plan. Successful participation exercises generally involve a range of initiatives that can include:

- household, visitor and business survey questionnaires;

- exhibitions;

- meetings and workshops (designed to stimulate involvement); and

- informative newsletters or leaflets.

Ideally consultation with residents, retailers and other bodies should be undertaken at a number of key stages in the planning process. The emphasis of the first stage should be on:

- the need for improvements and change;

- evaluation of the problems which should be addressed;

- the broad solutions available; and

- the wider implications of each solution in terms of cost and impact.

Following public participation it may be necessary to amend the business/action plan before the selected project option is selected. Design details should only be considered in the later stages of the consultation process.

Examples of Good Practice
Darlington

The implementation of streetscape improvements in Darlington was underpinned by a comprehensive consultation exercise. Information was disseminated in leaflets to all 40,000 households in the borough. In addition talks and publicity events were held. An exhibition was arranged and questionnaires were completed by the public on design and landscape issues. In addition, substantial involvement on the scheme was carried out with traders in the area.

Windsor

The pedestrianisation of Peascod Street in Windsor had been considered desirable for a number of years. An initial consultation exercise (leaflet and questionnaire) indicated wide support for a move towards pedestrianisation (77% in favour). The outline concept was endorsed during the District Local Plan process and a detailed transport study. Potential solutions, within clearly identified physical parameters, were sought via an organised design competition.

This project team worked closely with trader and heritage groups, the police and bus operators. A second phase of public consultation was undertaken following the production of detailed designs, including another leaflet and questionnaire and a 'roadshow'. Regular feedback to traders and the public throughout the process helped to minimise disruption and uncertainty.

IMPLEMENTATION

In many ways the implementation stage of any project is the most critical not only in terms of the quality of preparation and workmanship, but also how local businesses and the public will view the success of the scheme in the future. Project overruns or other problems during implementation can undermine general levels of satisfaction, and it can take a long time for bad feelings amongst disgruntled businesses to subside.

It is vital that businesses and the public affected are kept informed. The establishment of a *project office* within the town centre and the appointment of a *project co-ordinator* are desirable. The project officer should act as a single point of contact, keeping all concerned informed, ensuring the appropriate level of publicity and monitoring the quality of construction.

Evidence from the case study towns indicates that the implementation of paving and other town centre environmental works can in some circumstances have a detrimental impact on pedestrian flows and trading performance. Disruption during implementation works can be severe. Therefore, the implementation process should be as short as possible and always avoid peak trading periods.

Publicity and Monitoring

Information should be available throughout the implementation of the scheme, including details of any obstructions caused by the works. This information should be available to the public and business and should be clear, concise and placed in a position to give adequate warning and notice.

Project supervision and monitoring by the project co-ordinator is essential to ensure that a high quality of workmanship is delivered. At all stages of construction the works need to be adequately inspected and approved.

THE LAUNCH

Given that urban space improvements can be very disruptive from both the retailer and shopper perspective, it can be beneficial to formally launch the completed scheme. This launch will help to demonstrate to all concern that the disruption is over. It also provides an excellent opportunity to promote the centre as a whole to a wide audience.

MANAGEMENT AND MAINTENANCE

As indicated earlier, the ongoing management and maintenance of the enhanced or newly created urban spaces should be considered carefully throughout the planning process. The continuing role of the steering group and project team is essential. They need to play some part in the formation of a dedicated maintenance team. The ongoing care of the scheme should not be merely handed over and forgotten. The involvement of officers/departments involved in maintenance and cleaning is required at an early stage in the process. The preparation of maintenance manuals setting out required quality standards which can be reviewed annually will help to ensure that the benefits of the improvements are maximised. This manual should incorporate maintenance procedures for the scheme plus details of the materials used and suppliers. For ongoing repairs and larger reinstatement work a supply of material should be set aside. This is specifically important when materials are not regularly available.

Local authorities should not only budget for ongoing cleaning and maintenance of their schemes but should also budget for renewal costs at the end of the effective lifecycle of the scheme. The adoption of an agreed maintenance strategy which has the commitment of all departments concerned within the relevant council authorities and town centre management company is essential to the ongoing success of the scheme.

Example of Good Practice
Bradford
The strategy for Bradford City Centre "The Heart of the Matter" proposed that highways, cleansing and grounds maintenance for the city centre required a separate budget which was allocated on the basis of higher standards. A series of other recommendations were also made relating to the timing and standards of maintenance work. In line with these proposals, a city centre maintenance team was established. Their budget for 1995/96 was £65,000 and this budget has been maintained for 1996/97. The dedicated budget and team have improved standards and the timing of maintenance in Bradford City Centre.

MONITORING PERFORMANCE

A monitoring programme designed to identify the short, medium and long term impact and benefits of the scheme should be put in place. This programme should specify performance targets and should help to identify emerging problems and any modifications required. It can also help to quantify success, which may increase support for subsequent phases of work.

Monitoring the performance of improvement schemes and wider town centre management initiatives should be undertaken at regular intervals (2-3 years) as part of the town centre monitoring process advocated in PPG6, in particular the main measures of vitality and viability listed in PPG6. The ongoing monitoring process will ultimately feed into to the next major review of the development plan and the town centre strategy.

CHAPTER 7
Case Study Towns and Schemes

Case Study Evaluation

Interviews were held with the relevant local authority officers involved in the planning and implementation of the urban space enhancement schemes. These interviews were used to obtain details of the case study town and the enhancement schemes undertaken, including information which demonstrated the main achievements of the scheme. A number of issues were explored, including:

- before and after evidence of success (subjective and objective);

- problems that initiated the decision to implement the schemes and how these problems were tackled;

- how the problems and remedies were initially identified and evaluated;

- how the views of the general public, retailers, landowners and other interested parties were ascertained;

- how the balance between cost, quality and value for money were considered; and

- lessons learnt and how, with hindsight, those things which may have been done differently.

Visits to the case study towns were undertaken in order to:

- gain an understanding of the measures implemented and the problems they have sought to address; and to

- assess through observation the degree of success, in terms of pedestrian movement, non-essential use of urban spaces, quality of the environment, cleanliness and the durability of materials.

The remainder of this section summarises the evaluation of each case study town, and highlights the main lessons for good practice.

ABERDEEN – CITY CENTRE PROJECT

THE GOOD PRACTICE CASE

The creation and enhancement of public spaces within Aberdeen City Centre was successfully linked with wider regeneration and development initiatives. A joint public and private sector initiative addressed the declining physical fabric within the city centre, which has had broad ranging benefits, and has generated significant private sector leverage.

Aberdeen had thrived as a major regional centre. Historically, Union Street was the primary shopping area, but the development of major covered shopping centres in the 1980's, the St Nicholas and Bon Accord centres, shifted the primary area to the north of Union Street. Environmental measures since 1990 have attempted to redress this imbalance. The use of local granite and natural stone is in keeping with Aberdeen's historical character and has produced high quality and durable public spaces, although lower cost materials have been used in less sensitive areas.

Key Issues

By the late 1980's the levels of dilapidation and dereliction in the city centre were major concerns. A lack of residential accommodation and declining population was identified within the central area. In addition, spaces between buildings required attention. There was a lack of quality public spaces within the city centre where people could sit and rest. A partnership initiative between the City and Regional Councils, Grampian Enterprise and Scottish Homes targeted these problems.

The Scheme

The partnership has jointly implemented a number of regeneration projects throughout the city centre since 1991. Residential redevelopment schemes have helped to improve rundown areas. Many of these schemes have incorporated streetscape enhancement proposals. The main streetscape improvements, include:

- pedestrianisation of St. Nicholas Street which links Union Street and a covered shopping centre;

- the creation of 'pocket' parks, general landscaping and street furniture improvements around the city centre;

- extension and improvements to the paved Castlegate area; and

- enhancement of the Green including the refurbishment of derelict properties and improvements to the Market.

Process and Implementation

The problems of dereliction and poor quality public spaces were recognised in the late 1980s. A conceptual study of the city centre, drawing on the results from a public attitude survey was commissioned in 1990. This study identified a number of opportunities for enhancement, and highlighted the lack of quality public spaces. The local authorities, Grampian Enterprise and Scottish Homes formed the Aberdeen City Centre Partnership team which agreed a three year renewal programme and defined a city centre partnership area. A multi-disciplinary team was established to implement the programme.

The renewal programme combined the enhancement of urban spaces with wider urban regeneration objectives, in particular the re-use of derelict properties and the development of residential accommodation within the city centre. This approach enabled the partnership to secure private sector leverage. For example, residential development helped to fund environmental enhancement measures.

The Green, Aberdeen

Management and Maintenance

An on-going implementation programme has been agreed following the completion of the initial proposals, and a number of further schemes are currently being considered. A formal evaluation exercise is currently underway in order to monitor the strategy and to identify actual benefits. This evaluation exercise is expected to focus on economic indicators and the impact on investment decisions.

The Green

Castlegate

The formation of the City Centre Partnership has provided a more co-ordinated framework for the on-going management of the centre. The multi-disciplinary team formed to implement enhancement proposals continue to work closely and meet regularly. The implementation of CCTV has been a recent initiative.

Evaluation

The Aberdeen City Centre Project provides an excellent example of partnership working for city centre regeneration. It has demonstrated the important role that streetscape projects can have in influencing investment decisions.

Given, that the streetscape projects were only one element of a wider strategy, it is difficult to pinpoint or separate out the specific contribution that these urban space improvements have made. However, their impact on specific run-down areas has been significant.

Trading Performance

Aberdeen as a whole has performed well during the recession in comparison with other centres across the country. The role of physical improvements in maintaining Aberdeen's vitality and viability is difficult to quantify, as many of the schemes relate to specific, often secondary, areas within the city centre. Undoubtedly, these improvements have played a part in the overall success of Aberdeen.

Property Investment

The City Centre Project has implemented a large number of regeneration schemes, which have provided over 1,500 new homes within the city centre. In terms of commercial development the enhancement of the Green has provided an improved open air market and has redeveloped derelict buildings to provide new shop units.

Social Benefits

The streetscape elements of the wider City Centre Project have improved the provision of public spaces in and around the city centre, and have significantly upgraded the aesthetic quality of run down areas. The pedestrianisation of St Nicholas Street, although a small area in the context of the city centre as a whole, has provided a well used public space which has attracted street entertainment, and has improved pedestrian linkages.

AYR – TRAFFIC PLAN AND STREETSCAPE PROJECT

THE GOOD PRACTICE CASE

The Ayr Traffic Plan and Streetscape Project demonstrate how physical constraints can be overcome through the implementation of design and management measures. The relatively low cost scheme also shows the value of implementing temporary measures initially in order to test proposals and to avoid on-going disruption and uncertainty.

Ayr is the principal centre for industry, commerce and leisure in Ayrshire, attracting shopping visitors from a wide catchment area including many tourist visitors. A successful combination of measures and enhancement proposals was implemented in Ayr town centre to tackle fundamental congestion problems. These measures improved the shopping environment for visitors, whilst retaining vehicular access to the linear shopping area. The formation of a joint multi-disciplinary team was critical to the planning and implementation of the scheme, and provided a balance between practical engineering/traffic solutions and aesthetic design quality. The improvements were part of a wider town centre management initiative and action plan for Ayr town centre as a whole.

Key Issues

Ayr suffered like many other towns during the recession. Other problems included:

- increasing traffic, parked vehicles and narrow pavements which led to congested streets and pavements;

- the fabric of town centre had deteriorated due to the lack of investment; and the

- the impact of out-of-town centre retail developments had drawn trade from the town centre.

The Scheme

Pedestrianisation of the High Street was impractical due to the lack of rear servicing and the linear nature of the street. The Traffic Plan and Streetscape Project introduced a pedestrian priority scheme, which incorporated a new one way system in the previously congested High Street, allowing pavements to be widened and enhanced. Access to the High Street was restricted to buses, authorised taxis, the disabled and service vehicles. Other vehicles are encouraged to use the inner ring road. Traffic calming measures, frequent crossing points and bays for buses, taxis and service vehicles were provided to ensure an accessible but pedestrian friendly and safe environment. The mixture of materials used and the retention of a kerbed 'blacktop' carriageway have helped to minimise pedestrian/driver confusion. Pavement widening created opportunities for new public art with a local 'Rabbie Burns' theme and this has improved the aesthetic quality of the High Street.

The £1.4 million improvements were implemented through a three way partnership between Kyle and Carrick District Council, Strathclyde Regional Council and Enterprise Ayrshire. The partnership approach and broad improvements proposed were major factors in securing a contribution from the European Regional Development Fund. Other measures/improvements were required to enable the scheme to be implemented successfully, including a:

- voucher car parking scheme for on-street car parking;

- road junction capacity improvements to provide an inner ring road system;

- new pedestrian crossings and traffic lights;

- enhancements within pedestrianised side streets; and

- a shopmobility scheme, CCTV and improved road signs and finger posts.

Process and Implementation

The problems facing Ayr in the late 1980's were well recognised, and traffic surveys demonstrated the need for change.

However, opinions on potential solutions, particularly amongst local businesses, were divided during the Local Plan preparation process. Three broad options were initially put forward for debated and evaluation;

- no change;

- full pedestrianisation; and

- partial pedestrianisation.

Pedestrian priority scheme

These options and access issues were carefully debated by the District and Regional Councils and local businesses. During discussions and public meetings it was established that servicing would need to be retained via the High Street and that restricted servicing hours would be impractical. Furthermore, the exclusion of public transport and taxi within the linear high street would undermine accessibility. As a result pavement widening and one-way restricted access emerged as the preferred option. This option was exhibited and 40,000 leaflets were distributed. A second leaflet outlining detailed proposals was circulated prior to implementation.

The original Traffic Management Scheme was to be implemented in phases over a three year period. However, in an effort to avoid a long drawn out implementation period all changes were implemented at once. The practical implications of the scheme were tested following temporary arrangements in the High Street in 1993. The scheme was finally implemented after six years of preparation and consultation.

Management and Maintenance

Given the wide range of measures implemented in and around Ayr town centre, on-going management and maintenance during and after the implementation of the town centre action plan have been critical to the continued success of the scheme. A co-ordinated approach between the regional and district council, the police and the Ayr Town Centre Management Initiative has under-pinned this success.

Prior to the implementation a commitment was given by the all partnership members to review the performance of the scheme after a six month period. Various affected organisations and individuals were invited to give their views on the scheme and its operation. As a result a number of further improvements emerged and are currently being addressed. Many teething problems were experienced. However, the general consensus is positive.

Evaluation

The traffic management and streetscape proposals have had a significant impact on the quality of the environment and the level of safety within the High Street, whilst retaining accessibility. The commercial impact of the improvements has, as yet, not been dramatic. However, it has been important in helping Ayr to maintain its position in the shopping hierarchy during the recession, despite out-of-town centre retail developments and improvements in competing centres.

Property Investment
Although shop vacancies have not declined since the scheme was completed, they have remained stable in the face of increasing competition. The improvements have acted as a catalyst for shop improvements, store modernisation and re-fittings, including Boots, Marks and Spencer and Littlewoods. The refurbishment of Dalblair Arcade has also commenced.

Awards
1995 UK National Traffic Calming Award (Urban Street Environment Magazine)
1995 Street Design Competition (Local Government Magazine)
1995 Town Centre Environment Award (BCSC)

Property Values
Rental levels declined during the recession in Ayr but have now started to improve. Increases in rental levels have been attributed to a combination of the pedestrianisation scheme and wider regional improvements.

Safety and Security
The traffic calming measures have successfully reduced average speeds in the High Street to 17 miles per hour. As a result the average number of road accidents has reduced from over 20 to 1 per annum. Strathclyde Police have indicated that the scheme and CCTV measures have significantly reduced crime levels .

Enhanced streetscape, Ayr High Street

Retained Bus and service access, Ayr High Street

Social Benefits

The scheme has significantly enhanced the shopping environment for pedestrians and has improved the use of public spaces. The examination of before and after video pictures clearly demonstrates the operational improvements. Congestion within the High Street has been removed. Traffic flows during the day and evenings have declined by approximately 80%.

The new traffic and management arrangements have included the provision of designated disabled car parking in the central area. The voucher parking system has proved to be simple and has ensured the availability of short stay spaces.

BOURNEMOUTH – TOWN SQUARE

THE GOOD PRACTICE CASE

Budgetary constraints postponed the implementation of Bournemouth Borough Council's plans to close a major roundabout within the town centre to create a new town square. However, the council recognised that alternative measures were required to alleviate constraints to pedestrian movement across the town centre.

The low cost interim solution has created an effective and attractive pedestrian route and a popular public space. The council have also retained the option of implementing the full scheme, if funding becomes available in the future. The scheme demonstrates that temporary or partial solutions can be successful and significantly more desirable than the 'do nothing' scenario, particularly when one is faced with severe conflict problems between pedestrians and vehicles.

Key Issues

The primary retail area within Bournemouth town centre was effectively dissected by a roundabout linking the main shopping streets, Old Christchurch Road and Commercial Road. This roundabout also dissected the linear park which links the town centre and the seafront, hindering pedestrian movement. The subway system under the roundabout was uninviting.

The Scheme

Master plan proposals were drawn up to convert the roundabout into a new town square, involving comprehensive landscape works within the newly created public space and adjacent parks. These proposals would have involved the closure of the roundabout to traffic leaving an east-west route at the southern edge. However, the closure of the roundabout required the construction of a new bridge and link road to the north of the area. Due to a lack of funding an interim solution was prepared and implemented in 1992.

The interim (or temporary) solution involved only the partial closure of the roundabout, retaining east-west traffic on both sides of the roundabout. These traffic management measures enabled the creation of a new pedestrian link between the previously dissected shopping areas and established an attractive and popular public space. The potential remains to implement the full scheme in the future.

Process and Implementation

A traffic study identified that there was the potential to remove traffic from the roundabout. The parameters identified within the traffic study formed the basis of Local Plan policies to create the new town square in 1988. The scheme was widely supported by local traders, who were concerned that Bournemouth town centre would continue to decline if pedestrian linkages were not improved.

The council had limited in-house expertise to draw up detailed plans. Therefore, a national design competition was undertaken to select a suitable scheme. Design consultancies were invited to submit concept designs within stipulated physical and functional parameters. Specialist landscape advisors were used to evaluate each scheme. Each submission was also exhibited to assess the views of the public and traders. The preferred scheme was selected on the basis of design quality and public opinion. As a result the cheapest solution was not selected.

New town square and improved pedestrian linkages

However, funding was not available to progress the construction of the full scheme, including the provision of a new link road and bridge. The Council decided to prepare a low cost (£280,000) in-town solution and Traffic Regulation Orders were used to close the roads on a experimental basis prior to implementation. The option to implement the full scheme at a later date is retained and potential sources of funding are currently being investigated.

Management and Maintenance

Responsibility for care and maintenance of the roundabout was previously with the county highways department.

The conversion of the roundabout into a new public space has required different management and maintenance arrangements. The public space is now maintained by the borough council as part of the wider pedestrianised area within the town centre.

The popularity of the public space has created new management issues. The use of the area for entertainment needs to be controlled during peak periods, in order to avoid congestion.

The operation and success of the interim scheme have been carefully monitored, via traffic flow counts and video camera analysis. Public opinion surveys were also undertaken in 1993 and 1994 in order to gauge success. This evaluation work has provided evidence supporting the continuation of the interim scheme and has highlighted the ultimate benefits of the implementation of the full scheme.

Evaluation

The creation of the town square has proved to be extremely popular with visitors and shoppers within the town. Visitor surveys indicate that 95% of respondents believed the scheme is an improvement on the previous situation. The public space created has also proved to be very popular with pedestrians providing an attractive area to stop and sit. The area is also used by street entertainers and for events. In some respects the square has become a victim of its own success, as it can become crowded.

The economic signs within the town centre are also positive, which suggest that the changes have contributed to the recovery of Bournemouth from the effects of the recession.

Trading Performance
Approximately, 70% of visitors interviewed in Bournemouth suggested that the changes would encourage them to visit the town centre more often. This implies that the scheme should have a positive impact on Bournemouth's trading performance. PMRS data suggest that overall pedestrian flows have improved by 9% between 1991 and 1994 within the town centre.
Feedback from retailers has also been positive. The changes have provided a much improved pedestrian link between the two primary shopping areas. Indeed, many would like to see the implementation of the full scheme.

Property Values
Prime Zone A rental levels in Bournemouth town centre declined by approximately 20% in the early 1990's due to the recession, but have started to recover since the scheme was implemented. Investment yields have also improved.

Safety & Security
The changes have improved the perceived level of safety, as pedestrians do not have to use the subways. In addition, surface level pedestrian crossing has been made significantly easier and safer. Approximately, 97% of visitors suggested that the area was easy to cross.

Social Benefits
The changes have created an attractive and usable public space. A large majority (94%) of visitors indicated that they thought the scheme was attractive.

BRADFORD – CENTRAL AREA PEDESTRIANISATION

THE GOOD PRACTICE CASE

The Bradford case study illustrates how a well conceived and implemented scheme must be managed over time to ensure that benefits to users are maintained. The use of high quality traditional materials in areas where there is very high pedestrian flow has prolonged the life of the pedestrianisation scheme which links the two main shopping areas of Broadway and Darley Street. However, the success of the project was threatened in the late 1980's due to the increase in access permits granted and the consequent conflict between vehicles and pedestrians. Strict management policies have now been enforced to restrict non-essential vehicles from entering the pedestrianised area. This has secured pedestrian priority in the centre of Bradford.

Key Issues

Pedestrianisation within Bradford's central area had a broad range of objectives, as follows:

- the linking of the two main shopping areas in Bradford City Centre with a pedestrian thoroughfare to create an attractive and relaxed environment for shoppers;

- to improve the attractiveness of Bradford City Centre in the wake of competition from Leeds, smaller towns such as Halifax and the out of town retail developments;

- to create a setting for the Grade 1 listed Wool Exchange to provide a major city centre asset;

- developing a pedestrian 'gathering' area outside the Wool Exchange at the intersection of six streets to create a new focus and to unify the area;

- to promote the city centre as a 'shop window' for the district, which needs to reflect quality and vitality.

The Scheme

The pedestrianisation scheme formed a major part of the Council-led initiative to regenerate Bradford City Centre. The inner ring road system, completed in the late 1980's, provided the authority with an opportunity to create a more attractive and traffic free environment for pedestrians in the city centre.

The scheme includes the City Centre Conservation Area and contains Ivegate and other traditional streets and Victorian buildings.

Pedestrianisation of the trafficked streets was seen as the obvious choice because of the steep slopes and narrow widths of the carriageways. The use of Yorkstone flags and granite setts together with the choice of street furniture and lighting all echo the Victorian age of the buildings. There are many historical references throughout the scheme, in particular, the Ivegate arch which forms a gateway to the pedestrianised area.

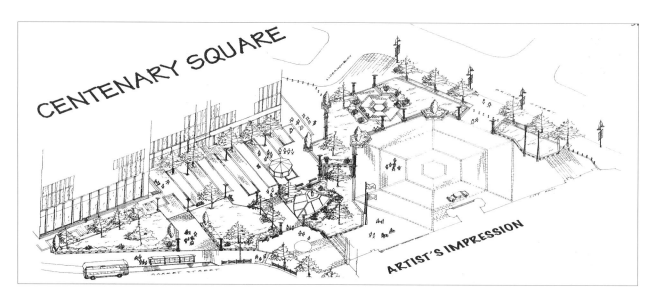

Process and Implementation

The scheme was implemented over an extended period between 1986 and 1989. Using Urban Programme money the pedestrianisation started with Ivegate and part of Bank Street while changes were made to Tyrell Street. The improvements were predominantly officer led, although proposals for the pedestrianisation were set out in the adopted City Centre Local Plan.

The project was managed by the Town Centre Team within the Council's Planning Division. Throughout implementation, initiatives were taken by the council without formal consultation with the business community. However, in recent years, the authority has adopted a partnership approach towards the implementation of new development proposals to ensure common ownership of projects.

This approach was considered to be the most appropriate to the City Centre Conservation Area. In contrast, more modern materials and street furniture have been used in the Broadway area.

Management and Maintenance

The capital scheme philosophy was to use traditional high quality materials which would last many years. So far one of the successes of the pedestrianisation scheme is its durability. However, during the late 1980's and early 1990's the scheme suffered from an uncoordinated approach to maintenance. As a result of this a strategy for Bradford City Centre "The Heart of the Matter" proposed that highways, cleansing and grounds maintenance for the city centre required a separate budget which should be allocated on the basis of higher standards.

There was a series of other recommendations relating to the timing and standards of maintenance work. In line with these proposals, a city centre maintenance team was established. Their budget for 1995/96 was £65,000 and this budget has been maintained for 1996/97. A dedicated budget and team have improved standards and the timing of maintenance in Bradford City Centre over the last two or three years, although more recently there have been protracted negotiations over the new maintenance contract.

Evaluation

The Bradford City Centre resurfacing scheme is a good example of an appropriate design solution to improve the environment for pedestrians and shoppers. This scheme has been in place since 1989 and demonstrates the value of high quality stone in re-paving schemes in terms of durability. This scheme is also a good example of the importance of management and good maintenance, irrespective of the initial quality of the materials used.

In particular, the re-assessment of access to parking permits and servicing hours, resulting in much tighter controls on access has ensured that the benefits of the scheme for pedestrians have been retained.

Property Investment

The trading benefits associated with these major infrastructure improvements have lagged behind the completion of the scheme, although significant refurbishment of major commercial buildings were triggered by the scheme. Major refurbishments oh the Grade 1 listed Wool Exchange and the adjoining Brown and Muff department store will be completed in 1996, introducing new quality retail.

The Major retail developments which were set to go ahead were abandoned due to the effect of the recession, which reduced trading performance in Bradford. Confidence in the city is returning and the development of 105,000 sq. ft of non-food retailing at Forster Square is due to be completed in Autumn 1996.

Property Values

Zone A rental reached a peak of £90 per sq. ft in 1991 shortly after the scheme was completed. However, rental levels have dropped since 1991 due to the recession in line with national trends.

Awards

Bradford City Centre pedestrianisation scheme was joint winner in the annual street design competition sponsored by Local Government News in 1989. In the same year, the scheme was also chosen for a Civic Trust award.

Social Benefits

The pedestrianisation of Bradford City Centre has had a range of environmental benefits for pedestrians and shoppers. The scheme has created safe and attractive areas for walking, sitting and browsing and has helped to reduce pedestrian's exposure to traffic pollution. The area now provides an attractive setting for street entertainment and the annual award winning Bradford Festival.

CARDIFF – CAFE QUARTER

THE GOOD PRACTICE CASE

The new *Cafe Quarter* at Mill Lane in Cardiff demonstrates how a run down secondary area can be transformed by urban space enhancement and careful theming. The key to success has undoubtedly been the effective partnership and close working between the business community and public agencies benefiting from wider city centre management networks and working practices. The project demonstrates what can be achieved when the public and private sectors work closely together to realise a shared goal at both strategic and action levels.

Plans to establish a new cafe quarter in Mill Lane emerged from local traders, who convinced the authorities to improve Mill Lane as part of a wider city centre investment strategy. The traders group succeeded in engaging in a partnership with the City and County Councils and the WDA, in order to make their idea a reality.

Mill Lane has been transformed into a continental style piazza, which provides a unique experience for residents, visitors and tourists alike. It has become the premier restaurant destination within the city centre.

Key Issues

Mill Lane was a decaying forgotten secondary shopping street on the southern fringe of Cardiff city centre.

Vacancy levels were high and many buildings were in a poor condition, despite the significant potential of the historic buildings in the area.

The development of a major hotel and other initiatives to regenerate the area in the 1980's and early 1990's were unsuccessful although restauranteurs had started to colonise the street.

The Scheme

Mill Lane was a three lane one-way carriageway with commercial premises on the northern side. The Cardiff Marriot Hotel is situated on the southern side of Mill Lane. The scheme involved pavement widening on the northern side, and the narrowing of the carriageway to one lane, with lay-bys for buses and taxis. The enlarged paved area now provides a substantial area for cafe tables and chairs.

The scheme was completed in June 1995. High quality natural paving slabs, granite sets and kerbs have been used. Specially designed decorative railings, banners, umbrellas and street lighting have be used to create a top quality environment with a Welsh flavour.

Mill Lane, 'before'

Mill Lane, 'after'

Revived 'evening economy'

High quality natural materials

Process and Implementation

Mill Lane café quarter was a business community driven concept. However, the enhancement scheme was one element of holistic strategy for Cardiff city centre.

This strategy, *Cardiff City Centre – Prospectus for Investment*, set out an agreed vision for Cardiff and identified key projects. It evolved from a City Centre Partnership Forum with representatives from the private sector, Cardiff City Council, the Welsh Development Agency and other public agencies.

The strategy was broad based including objectives for shopping, tourism, the arts and culture, the '24 Hour City' employment, transport, promotion and marketing. The lack of quality public spaces in the city centre emerged as a major issue and five public areas had been identified for improvement, although Mill Lane was not originally considered. However, in Mill Lane businesses mobilised support and persuaded the City Centre Forum to incorporate their scheme into the strategy. The Mill Lane enhancement scheme was an important step in meeting the wider strategy objectives for the city centre. It was designed to become a new component of Cardiff's tourism product, serving both visitors and local residents and helping to develop the 24 Hour City.

The evolution of the Mill Lane enhancement scheme involved close working between the business community and the public sector making full use of city centre management network and working practices. Regular meetings were held throughout the planning and design of the scheme, with the emphasis on joint decision making. The physical parameters for the scheme were agreed, i.e. coverage and traffic management implications.

These meetings enable all parties concerned to understand the implications of each option, and allowed an agreed solution to emerge. The proposed pavement widening scheme was fully tested prior to implementation. A temporary scheme was employed to examine how the scheme would work and to identify potential problems. Full participation of all stakeholders in the evolution of the scheme from concept through to design and implementation was a key factor underpinning the success and economic sustainability of the scheme. The procurement process successfully broke down barriers between the public and private sectors at all levels. This close working has engendered a strong feeling of pride and ownership.

Management and Maintenance

The strong sense of ownership amongst businesses has benefited the on-going maintenance and management of the area.

There is a commitment to a voluntary code of practice aimed at maintaining high standards. There is a shared responsibility in the on-going management, cleaning and maintenance of the street. The traders have formed an association which aims to co-ordinate the promotion and marketing of the cafe quarter. Working closely with public agencies a programme of events and publicity have been developed.

Evaluation

Mill Lane has undergone a significant transformation and has become a significant destination. It is recognised as 'Cardiff's Cafe Quarter' attracting large numbers of customers, particularly on fine Summer evenings. The economic impact of the scheme was assessed six months after completion by the City Council. Interviews with occupiers and property owners in Mill Lane have provided impressive results. The scheme has had a clear impact on the trading performance and property investment.

Trading Performance
The majority of restaurants recorded dramatic (120-500%) increases in turnover since the scheme was completed. Many restaurants have subsequently extended their opening hours. Some retailers indicated that a modest improvement in turnover had been achieved.

Property Investment
Direct investment as a result of the Mill Lane initiative has been estimated at around £4.5 million, from an £800,000 investment by the public sector. This spin-off investment included; new occupiers, refurbishment of premises and the adjacent Wyndham Arcade. The number of vacant units has fallen and there is currently only one vacant unit in Mill Lane.

Property Values
No rent reviews or sales have been undertaken in Mill Lane since the scheme was completed. However, property owners anticipate that values will increase significantly in the future.

Employment
An estimated additional 70 part-time jobs were created during the summer months.

Awards
Local Government News – Street Design competition
Winner Pedestrian Environment Category
RICS Award for Urban Renewal – shortlisted
RTPI Award for Planning Achievement – shortlisted

Social Benefits
The popularity of the initiative is clear evidence of success. Indeed, in some respects the area has been a victim of its own success. Managing the large numbers of customers and reducing congestion are issues which must be tackled in the future.

CONWY – PEDESTRIAN PRIORITY IN AN HISTORIC SETTING

THE GOOD PRACTICE CASE

Conwy is a unique historic town, with a castle and town walls which have been designated a world heritage site by UNESCO. It represents a good example of a town with multiple pressures in a constrained historic setting which has:

- achieved a balance between conservation and enhancement of the environment;
- maintained a thriving tourism industry; and
- respected and supported the interests of local residents and businesses.

A range of pedestrian priority and conservation projects have been implemented over the last ten years which have enhanced significantly the attractions of the town centre.

Key Issues
The opportunity to remove through traffic in Conwy town centre was created by the completion of the tunnel crossing the Conwy estuary, which improved accessibility to the national road network with the completion of the A55 Expressway. It also provided a number of opportunities to address other objectives within the town centre, including:

- improvements to the conservation, maintenance and enhancement of the historic fabric of buildings;
- the creation of a predominantly traffic free environment by accommodating visitor and long stay parking outside the town in peak periods;
- the development of a co-ordinated marketing programme;
- the creation of pedestrianised areas and accompanying environmental improvements which harmonise with the towns historic fabric;
- helping to reduce the number of vacant shop units in the central core.

Preserving Conwy's historic character

Complementary natural materials

The Scheme

Many of the improvement schemes which took place during the early 1990's were funded by the Town Scheme. Under this scheme, property making a contribution to the character of the conservation area is eligible for grant, normally 50% towards approved costs of repair, preservation or restoration. During this period, public sector funding was £50,000 per annum for five years which ensured that these schemes were implemented. The Town Scheme is still in operation, although at a lower level of funding. The first improvements undertaken were not funded by the Town Scheme, and included the resurfacing of Church Street in 1992, an important shopping street approaching St Mary's Church but was not.

This scheme has large setts and brick paving, although the original layout has been retained. The Lancaster Square enhancement took place in 1993 and the aim was to create a civic space and public gathering area in the town where there was previously a tarmac car park. The roadways were resurfaced with setts, edged with stone kerbs and pedestrian areas were completely re-paved with natural stone.

The High Street is the principal shopping street in Conwy town centre. This was developed as a pedestrian priority area in 1994, which can be closed to traffic during special events. Some pavement areas were widened and the reduced roadway was resurfaced with Yorkstone slabs, edged with stone kerbs while the pavements were flagged with Yorkstone. During 1995, enhancements to Castle Street were carried out which included widening of the pavements and resurfacing.

Process and Implementation

The catalyst for the improvements to Conwy town centre was the opening of the tunnel crossing the estuary in 1991. Once the scheme was secured, the potential for the removal of through traffic in the town centre was seen as a major opportunity for the development of a new strategy for Conwy.

Consultants were appointed by a number of public bodies (Aberconwy Borough Council, Cadw, Conwy Town Council, Gwynedd County Council, National Trust, WTB and the WDA), and a strategy for the future incorporating an action plan was published in 1988. Many of the recommendations set out by the consultants were implemented in a process which involved members and officers jointly.

Management and Maintenance

The first phase of the scheme, Church Street re-paving, was carried out without the benefit of previous experience. Learning from their mistake the council decided to use natural materials for the other phases of work. The better quality finish is expected to result in lower maintenance costs and greater durability. All maintenance matters are covered by the council's general maintenance programme.

Evaluation

The implementation of the improvements in the town centre have acted as a catalyst for many other initiatives, both from private individuals and the public sector.

The general view of retailers in Conwy has been positive towards the improvement programme. The quality of the streetscape and shopping environment have been significantly improved.

Property Investment

Shop vacancy rates in Conwy have reduced since the early 1990's and more specialist shops have opened. Shop fronts have been refurbished, especially in High Street and hanging baskets have become a common feature in the central areas.

Awards
The Borough Council's scheme was overall winner in the 'Best Street Scene' category of the Wales Tourist Board signage competition in 1994.

Social Benefits
The pedestrian priority schemes in the town centre have improved conditions for shoppers and visitors alike. The creation of the civic space at Lancaster Square has given the town centre a resting place and a destination for pedestrians, which is very well used throughout the year.

Complementary streetscape improvements such as traditional lighting, fingerposts and street furniture have combined to give the town centre a quality ambience and appeal.

COVENTRY – CITY CENTRE REGENERATION

THE GOOD PRACTICE CASE

The enhancement of existing pedestrianised areas within Coventry city centre has been an important factor in the successful regeneration strategy for the centre as a whole. These urban space enhancement proposals were part of a broader strategy for the city centre. The success of the strategy was under-pinned by:

- a detailed preliminary evaluation of the city centre;

- wide ranging objectives addressing many of city centre's functions;

- close working between the public and private sector; and

- structured on-going monitoring, maintenance and management.

The City Council used the private sector's development and management expertise to construct a comprehensive action orientated regeneration strategy. Indeed Coventry pioneered many management initiatives which have now been widely adopted. The strategy recognised that change would not be immediate and that a long term and incremental approach needed to be adopted. The implementation of this strategy is an excellent example of phased improvements delivered through a multi-agency and partnership approach.

Key Issues
Coventry city centre was redeveloped after World War II, and was at the time a national showpiece. However, the centre declined during the 1980's due to the lack of investment, reduced commercial confidence and greater competition from neighbouring centres and out-of-town retail schemes. The pedestrianised precincts had become rundown, sub-standard and unattractive for shopping. The regeneration strategy targeted these problems by focusing on providing:

- a good range and balance of facilities;

- ease and convenient access;

- an attractive and secure environment;

- good management, promotion and entertainment; and a

- user friendly centre.

The Lower Precinct, the next piece of the jigsaw

The Scheme
The regeneration strategy was a comprehensive package of initiatives designed to improve the overall image of Coventry to investors, visitors and local residents. However, the emphasis initially was focused on achieving better management, the enhancement of the public realm and tackling public safety concerns. The partnership implemented phased re-paving between 1990 to 1994, in order to upgrade the quality of the ageing shopping precincts. A fountain provides a focal point at the intersection of the four precincts. Traffic calming measures were also implemented around the city centre to improve pedestrian access. The re-development of the Lower Precinct will be the remaining piece in the jigsaw.

Water Fountain, a new focal point

Shelton Square

Town centre management measures adopted prior to the public realm improvements provided an appropriate context for success and the on-going maintenance of the centre, including:

- the formation of a City Centre Management Team;

- CCTV installation;

- the formation of an Alcohol and Crime Project Group;

- a shopmobility scheme; and

- car park improvements.

The urban space enhancement proposals were incorporated in a wider package of initiatives including the provision of a library, leisure and other community facilities.

Process and Implementation

The regeneration strategy for Coventry was supported by comprehensive preparatory work. The importance of measuring and understanding the existing performance of Coventry city centre was recognised. Detailed information was collated and analysed including; footfall counts, car park usage, vacancies, crime levels and private sector perceptions. A study of the city centre was commissioned which highlighted Coventry's problems and the need for short and long term action.

The successful evaluation of these problems and the identification of potential solutions was underpinned by survey analysis to establish the views of:

- potential investors;

- local residents;

- local businesses; and

- visitors to Coventry.

This evaluation confirmed that the image of Coventry was a critical issue, and that the quality and management of the environment was a major factor. This work formed a sound basis for the emerging City Centre Strategy and Action Plan. Concept proposals were prepared for public consultation. The formation of a partnership company between the City Council and the private sector helped the on-going strategy and annual business plans to be realised. It also helped to secure private sector funding contributions for the implementation of the strategy, which in turn helped to secure substantial European funding. The background work allowed the partnership to move quickly to secure this funding. Priorities were quickly identified and a phased approach was adopted (four main phases). The partnership structures, background work and the existence of the agreed strategy enabled Coventry to prepare a credible bid at short notice.

Management and Maintenance

Coventry's long standing Safe and Clean campaign and the introduction of town centre management and CCTV provided an excellent basis for maximising the potential of the precinct areas through enhancement measures. The existing partnership approach to town centre management, maintenance, cleaning and promotion have helped to ensure high quality street surfaces and maximum utilisation of urban spaces. The Partnership company have adopted performance standards for contractors and plan to produce a detailed maintenance manual. An on-going budget for renewal has been secured and a clear view of the lifespan (15 years) of the enhancement scheme were established prior to implementation. Through these mechanisms the community are encouraged to organise activities in the public spaces to increase the appeal of the centre to users.

Evaluation

The regeneration strategy has undoubtedly transformed the quality of the environment and public spaces, introducing new activities and events. The image of Coventry and the level of civic pride has improved significantly. However, attitudes and past perceptions will take a considerable time to change. The commercial benefits of the public space and management measures are difficult to isolate, given that other initiatives and private sector investment have also improved the city centre. However, the wider strategy has been successful.

Trading Performance

Major retailers have reported increased trade and customers from a wider area, with shops out performing branches in surrounding towns. These reports are supported by increases in footfall counts (up 3.5% on week days and up 25% on Saturdays) and short stay car park usage (up 30% since 1990). However, evidence does suggest that the disruption during implementation was detrimental to trading levels.

Property Investment

The package of proposed initiatives was an important catalyst for major private sector investment in the form of new shopping centres at West Orchard and Cathedral Lanes. The two shopping developments have been relatively successful. Voids within the precinct areas increased during the early 1990's due in part to the opening of the West Orchard shopping centre. However, voids in the improved areas of the precinct area have now declined and vacancy levels are very low.

Property Values

A resurgence in rental levels has occurred in Coventry due to a combination of the enhancement schemes and an improved property market nationally. Rental levels are now comparable to peak 1989 levels. Fringe retail re-development has recently taken place. Property yields have improved slightly faster than the national situation.

Safety & Security

The city centre has become one of the safest areas in Coventry. All forms of crime levels have fallen dramatically (30-40% reduction since 1990). CCTV in conjunction with Retail Radio Link have been instrumental in reducing vandalism and theft. The installation of clear signage and removal of pavement obstacles have served to enhance shoppers' perceptions of safety. The City has attracted 13 'Secure Car Park Awards' with a significant fall in car related crime.

Social Benefits

The popularity of the improved public spaces is evidence of success. New paving and the addition of a fountain have visibly improved the use of public spaces.

DARLINGTON – REFURBISHMENT SCHEMES

THE GOOD PRACTICE CASE

The refurbishment of central areas of Darlington was important to make the town more attractive and to enable it to compete with other local centres. Darlington is surrounded by quality shopping environments: MetroCentre at Gateshead, Newcastle to the north and York to the south and has responded to this high level of competition.

The comprehensive improvements undertaken in Darlington have been phased over a number of years and have integrated the central shopping area to form a cohesive whole. Pedestrians can now walk comfortably from the Market Place, across High Row through the Yards to Skinnergate, cutting across some historic and very attractive townscapes.

Key Issues

Competing shopping facilities within the North East had improved significantly. In comparison, Darlington did not offer an attractive environment for shoppers. In response to these problems the council sought to:

Darlington, 'before'

An enhanced environment for pedestrians

- improve conditions for pedestrians throughout the town centre;

- link the main shopping areas;

- create a high quality public open space at Market Place with direct access to the existing open market;

- increase the range of public events held in the town centre; and

- improve the general environment with particular emphasis on landscaping and seating.

The Scheme

The pedestrianisation, re-paving and landscaping of Skinnergate in March 1992 was the first major element of the improvement works to be undertaken.

Skinnergate is closed to traffic from 10.30am to 4pm and all deliveries take place outside these hours. Problems of traffic congestion and poor conditions for pedestrians had dominated Skinnergate. Investment in the area was declining and there was an increase in vacancy rates amongst independent retailers which undermined Skinnergate's character and vitality. The scheme also attempted to minimise the potential impact of the Cornmill redevelopment and out-of-town developments on the Skinnergate area.

The Yards which linked Skinnergate to High Row, the main shopping thoroughfare, were re-paved during the early 1990's, in recognition of their importance to pedestrians. The Yards are narrow arcades which are closed to through traffic. Changes to Market Place were controversial as the area was used as a car park on most days of the week, and as part of the proposals was turned into open space. Full pedestrianisation, upgrading and resurfacing of the Market Place was completed in April 1996. The car park on Market Place has been replaced with the addition of 87 parking spaces at the back of the town hall nearby.

Process and Implementation

In the run up to the 1991 elections there was considerable interest in the improvement of the town centre for visitors and shoppers from members and much of the impetus for change has been generated by politicians. Darlington Borough Council have a strong commitment to town centre management and the links between planning, transportation and town centre management are very strong. Throughout the process of planning and implementation, the authority sought to inform the public and the business community of the practicalities of the schemes.

With the redevelopment of Market Place, which required planning permission, there was an opportunity for the dissemination of information in leaflets to all 40,000 households in the borough, talks and publicity events. An exhibition was arranged and questionnaires were completed by the public on design and landscape issues. In addition, consultation on the scheme was carried out with traders in the area. All the pedestrianisation/traffic proposals were implemented on an experimental basis which allowed for full monitoring and evaluation of the schemes in practice.

Management and Maintenance

The management and maintenance issues relating to the schemes have not been fully developed to date. High quality materials were used in all locations, including heat treated sandstone pavements in Skinnergate and the re-paving of the Market area with granite setts. These materials were chosen in order to ensure the maximum durability of the resurfaced areas and minimise maintenance costs. Planning Officers have prepared a report for members on the management of the Market Place (April 1996). Recommendations include the formulation of a programme of recreational, social, cultural and leisure events to complement the twice weekly open market.

The report suggests that there may be a number of uses which will not be acceptable, including second hand car auctions or car boot sales. Day-to-day management and control issues centre around loading and parking restrictions in Market Place and their enforcement, particularly on market days. Revenue for maintenance is expected to be the responsibility of the town centre manager.

Evaluation

This scheme is a good example of the benefits of removing vehicles from shopping areas and allowing pedestrian access during core shopping hours. The knock on effects have been substantially reduced traffic flows in surrounding streets both inside and outside core shopping hours. Market research consultants were commissioned to assess public attitudes to the Skinnergate scheme during the experimental period, which demonstrated that the scheme is successful.

The results of the consultation and publicity for the re-paving of Market Place resulted in over 100 written responses, the vast majority of which were positive in their support for the principles of improvement. Only 16 responses constituted outright objections, which were mainly on the grounds of 'a waste of money' and 'loss of parking'.

Trading Performance
Before and after pedestrian counts were conducted in July 1991 and July 1992 in Skinnergate and the surrounding areas. The results showed that combined pedestrian counts (Friday and Saturday) increased by 14% after pedestrianisation

Property Values
Skinnergate is now considered to be good secondary shopping location and rents achieved in 1995 were about £30 per sq. ft zone A. Recent transactions on High Row have achieved rents of around £44 per sq. ft zone A.

Social Benefits
The pedestrianisation and refurbishment schemes have achieved many social benefits. These range from improved access for pedestrians, greater safety for shoppers, more seating and landscaping in busy shopping areas. Market Place has created the only large public space in the town centre which is traffic free and, increasingly will be used for special events and tourist activities.

Research carried out in August 1992 concluded that 87% of the public supported the principle of closing Skinnergate and High Road to traffic during the day, and 89% of respondents believed that the changes had made the area safer for pedestrians. Approximately 90% of the public believed that pedestrianisation had made the area a more pleasant shopping environment. Similar results were achieved from the business survey conducted at the same time, although more businesses were against the principle of closing Skinnergate to traffic (25% of all businesses in the area). However, only a minority (20%) of businesses questioned believed that the pedestrianisation should not be made permanent.

DERBY – THE PROMENADE

THE GOOD PRACTICE CASE

The Derby Promenade has transformed the heart of Derby, creating traffic free areas for people to enjoy during their visit to the city centre. The scheme has created extensive traffic free areas with seating, planting and public art. It has helped to create themed areas within the City Centre, including specialist shopping, cultural and commercial quarters.

The scheme emerged from the results of a comprehensive study of the City Centre, which provided the Council with a clear understanding of the problems faced by Derby. The changes were implemented in four phases between 1991 and 1994, minimising disruption. The renewal of underground services during construction further reduced disruption. Leaflets and other literature were regularly produced to keep the general public and local businesses fully informed.

The Derby City Centre Management Team, a partnership between the public sector and key city centre businesses, has built on the success of scheme. A number of management and promotional initiatives has

helped to make Derby more competitive. A range of accessibility measures has also been introduced to counter-balance the impact of the new traffic restriction areas.

Key Issues

The City Council commissioned a major shopping study for Derby. The study highlighted a number of weaknesses in the City Centre and indicated that Derby was losing out to competing centres. These weaknesses included; a poor overall environment, traffic congestion within important shopping streets, poor public spaces with inadequate street furniture and a general lack of private sector investment.

The Scheme

The proposals implemented in Derby City Centre have covered an extensive area. Traffic restrictions have been introduced within the main shopping area. Traffic has been removed during peak shopping hours. New paving and high quality lighting and street furniture have been provided.

The first phases of work involved the pedestrianisation of Sadler Gate and Iron Gate, followed by the major pedestrianisation and paving works within the primary shopping area, St Peter's Street and the Corn Market. The final phase involved the refurbishment, landscaping and provision of public art within the Market Place to provide a major focal point, suitable for exhibitions, specialist markets and other functions.

Man made materials appropriate to the City Centre's architecture have been used. However, high quality natural York stone has been used in sensitive areas within the Cathedral and within the Market Place.

Future accessibility to the main shopping area has been carefully addressed. A package of measures has been implemented including: new bus routes and stops, disabled car parking, taxi ranks, limited waiting zones, a shopmobility scheme and a park and ride scheme. A new bus station and multi-storey car park are also being planned as part of a major retail development.

Process and Implementation

Following the completion of the Derby shopping study, a multi-disciplinary officer working group from the City and County Councils prepared a 'plan of action' for the city centre designed to combat the weaknesses identified by the shopping study. This plan examined the potential for pedestrianising St Peter' Street and Albert Street. A transport study was also undertaken to address traffic management issues.

Following extensive consultation with retailers, businesses, transport operators and emergency services a draft scheme was prepared. The public consultation exercises demonstrated overwhelming support for the scheme. As a result, a revised scheme was produced. Given the large coverage of the proposed improvements a phased approach was adopted in order to minimise disruption.

Heavy traffic in St Peter's Street, before implementation

Pedestrianisation in Derby, after implementation

Management and Maintenance

The shopping study prepared prior to the improvements recommended the appointment of a City Centre Manager in Derby in order to build on other proposed improvements. The Council now have a City Centre Manager working with local businesses, helping to ensure that the benefits of the major investment are maximised. A Business Plan for the City centre has been produced and endorsed by the City Centre Management Team. This approach emphasises the need to attract new shoppers and to encourage new investment in the City Centre.

The Council hope to broaden this initiative through the formation of a City Centre Forum, establishing further links between the public and private sector. The Management Team is looking to retain more control over the use of public spaces. The new and enhanced spaces are viewed as an important asset which need to be managed in order to generate revenue for the City Centre from events, festivals and market stalls.

This revenue will be used to fund marketing and other activities to promote Derby City Centre. The City Centre Manager also provides a vital point of contact for the various agencies and contractors involved in the cleaning and maintenance of the City Centre. A City Centre Ranger has been employed by the Management Team, and is now working with the Council to secure new investment in the City Centre. There is already evidence of success, with the recently completed £15 million Albion Street shopping development, and there is growing interest from developers in other sites.

Evaluation

The environmental improvements undertaken in Derby and the comprehensive package of management initiatives have been widely viewed as very successful. The commercial and social benefits of the scheme have been demonstrated by public and business attitude surveys.

Derby appears to have performed relatively well during the last 5 years, despite the effects of the recession and increasing competition.

Trading Performance

PMRS pedestrian flowcounts for Derby indicate that overall pedestrian counts fell by over 20% between 1985 and 1991. However, flows improved by over 15% between 1991 and 1994.

A shopping study prepared in 1995 after the scheme had been implemented suggested that most existing retailers were optimistic about future trading patterns in Derby.

Property Investment

Derby has attracted an impressive list of new retailers since the scheme was completed including, Virgin Records, Disney, Oasis and Waterstones. Major refurbishments by existing retailers have also been completed including; C&A, BHS Littlewoods, Boots, Marks and Spencer and Principles. There has also been greater interest in grants for shop refurbishments. Interest in potential development sites within the City Centre has also re-emerged.

Property Values

Zone A rental levels reached a peak in 1990 (£90 per sq. ft), but dropped to £75 during the recession. Rental levels have improved slightly since the improvements were completed in 1994. Property yields have also improved.

Safety & Security

Crime levels (theft, criminal damage and attacks) remained relatively stable after the scheme was completed. However, the introduction of CCTV has helped to remove crime 'black spots' within the city centre and cars parks, and has reduced overall crime throughout the centre.

Social Benefits

A public attitude survey in 1995 indicated that there was a high level of satisfaction with the changes. Over 75% expressed satisfaction with the new pedestrianised areas and, over 65% commented on the cleanliness of the city centre. Retailers were generally happy with the scheme, although there were some concerns that there had been a perceived shift in focus to the south of the City Centre.

Statistics also show that the general air quality has improved in recent years.

ELGIN – HISTORIC CORE ENHANCEMENT

THE GOOD PRACTICE CASE

Urban space enhancement measures have helped to restored the historic character of Elgin town. The mediaeval street plan of Elgin is well preserved. Thereforee, the implemention of high quality and sympathetic improvements was essential. The careful choice of natural materials based on historic use has provided a finish that is durable, resistant to heavy goods service vehicles, attractive and appropriate in terms of colour and texture. The phased approach to implementation prevented this quality being compromised despite strict budgetary constrains.

The successful schemes is the outcome of 18 months of consultation, negotiation and careful consideraion of all users' requirements. The production of a number of study topic reports and the formation of Working and Forum Groups provided the appropriate basis for preparing and implmeneting the scheme.

Key Issues

Although the town relief road had removed most of the through traffic from the High Street in Elgin a high level of congestion remained within the historic cores. Traffic was directed around St Giles Church creating an island within the centre of the High Street.

The restriction of traffic from this widened section of the High Street presented an opportunity to restore the market place into an attractive and pleasant area for pedestrians. However, the proposals had major implications for public transport, traffic management and parking. Restricted access could not be implemented without altering existing traffic arrangements in outlying streets and the retention of servicing access.

The Scheme

Elgin High Street, around St Giles Church, has been re-paved using granite setts and local sandstone flags that match the materials used historically in Elgin.

The re-paved pedestrianised area has restricted delivery access outside peak shopping times and access for a limited number of permit holders. Car parking has been provided for the disabled at the gateways to the pedestrianised areas, and a 'shopmobility' scheme was introduced. A comprehensive restructuring of traffic management arrangements were implemented in the surrounding streets.

Process and Implementation The Good Practice Case

Urban space enhancement measures have helped to restored the historic character of Elgin town centre. The mediaeval street plan of Elgin is well preserved. Therefore, the implementation of high quality and sympathetic improvements was essential. The careful choice of natural materials based on historic use has provided a finish that is durable, resistant to heavy goods service vehicles, attractive and appropriate in terms of colour and texture. The phased approach to implementation prevented this quality being compromised despite strict budgetary constraints.

The successful scheme is the outcome of 18 months of consultation, negotiation and careful consideration of all users' requirements. The production of a number of study topic reports and the formation of Working and Forum Groups provided the appropriate basis for preparing and implementing the scheme.

Elgin High Street, before

Elgin High Street, after

Preserved mediaeval street plan

The concept of pedestrianisation in Elgin has been considered for many years following the completion of the town centre relief road in the 1970s. However, the need to retain service access and car parking within the central area made pedestrianisation difficult. The provision of off-street parking around the centre created an opportunity to re-examine the options for pedestrianisation. A town centre strategy was commissioned in 1989, which highlighted the reasons for Elgin's decline. Pedestrianisation was promoted by independent consultants as a potential improvement. A survey of 1,200 local people indicated that supporters of pedestrianisation outnumber those against by more than 5 times.

Four initial options were identified, including the retention of one-way or two way traffic one side of the Church. These options were presented to the public and were debated at meetings with interested parties. The majority were in favour of complete pedestrianisation around the St Giles Church. A limited version of the traffic management arrangements were tested prior to implementation in 1990.

To solve immediate concerns about pedestrian safety, a first phase of work was undertaken by the Regional Council in 1992, involving the extension of paved areas using concrete slabs. However, following further evaluation the decision to use lower cost man-made materials was reversed. A multi-disciplinary team of council officers produced a revised implementation strategy in 1993, following considerable background research, including:

- study tours of other towns/schemes;

- the production of comprehensive town centre topic reports;

- material and design tests, particularly for the blind and disabled; and a

- cost benefit analysis of the use of more costly natural materials.

This analysis underpinned the decision to use only durable natural materials, with a very long lifespan.

Management and Maintenance

The implementation strategy addressed the issues of future management and maintenance, highlighting the need to establish and reinforce responsibilities. It also identified the need to introduce a maintenance plan and legislative measures and programmes to ensure the on-going success of the scheme, including; a shop front guide, legalisation and guidance for the reinstatement of surfaces, a trained maintenance and management team and enhancement schemes for town centre properties.

Given that vehicular access for heavy goods servicing and other permit holders was to be retained, durable materials were required. Consideration was also given to the maintenance, replacement and cleaning of the chosen materials during the planning stage. The traffic management arrangements have been reviewed and amended since the scheme was implemented, following feedback from traders and private residents within the outlying streets. A survey has been undertaken to ascertain general views on the success of the scheme. The existence of a shopmobility scheme has helped to maintain accessibility for the disabled.

Evaluation

The measures implemented in Elgin are relatively new and the full impact and benefits remain unclear. However, preliminary analysis of public attitudes suggests that the scheme is very popular and successful. The initial detrimental impact on trading performance does not appear to be as severe as that experienced in other towns, which augers well for the future. The scheme has significantly improved the use of public spaces, and has encouraged street entertainment.

Trading Performance
It is probably too early to assess the full impact of the scheme on trading levels. However, a survey of

Market Place, 'the Plainstones'

shoppers indicated that 40% of shoppers interviewed said that they are more likely to shop in Elgin than before. If correct this would suggest a significant positive impact of trading performance. Although, some small traders on the periphery of the scheme have indicated that the traffic restrictions have been detrimental to their trade.

Pedestrian flowcounts shortly before and after the scheme was implemented suggest that footfall has remained relatively stable despite disruption during construction. Higher pedestrian flows and spending have been recorded within the St Giles Centre.

Property Investment

The planning and implementation of the schemes appears to have had a positive impact on property investment. The number of vacant shop premises in Elgin town centre reduced marginally between 1991 and 1996, despite the development of over 40 new units within St Giles Shopping Centre. The letting of units within the St Giles Shopping Centre has been relatively successful during a recessionary period.

The scheme costing £900,000 has acted as a catalyst for building repairs to properties within the High Street, and represents excellent value for money.

Safety & Security

The number of road accidents has decreased within the High Street, and perceived safety amongst shoppers has improved. Approximately 65% of shoppers felt that Elgin town centre provides a safe and secure environment (62% of women respondents). Additional lighting was introduced after the scheme in order to increase the feeling of securing. The possible introduction of CCTV is expected to further improve security.

Social Benefits

The social benefits of the scheme are clearly indicated by the results of shopper surveys. It has created an enhanced public arena and has stimulated civic pride. The survey of shoppers registered a high level of satisfaction (60-80%), with regard to appearance, shopping environment, events and lively atmosphere, lighting, security, safety and accessibility.

HEMEL HEMPSTEAD – PEDESTRIANISATION

THE GOOD PRACTICE CASE

The implementation of pedestrianisation in Hemel Hempstead demonstrates the importance of comprehensive prior planning and consultation. The resulting solution has provided an appropriate mix of full and partial pedestrianised areas and pavement widening, which reflect the role of specific areas within the town centre.

The measures implemented were undertaken in response to the severe problems faced by Hemel Hempstead and have transformed the town centre into a safer, more attractive environment predominantly for the use of pedestrians. These improvements have helped to minimise the impact of increasing competition from other nearby centres. The provision of public art has drawn attention away from the predominant 1960's architecture and has provided a clean and modern shopping environment. These benefits have been maximised by other town centre management initiatives already in place, and the scheme has been carefully monitored by a structured evaluation process.

Key Issues

The main shopping street in Hemel Hempstead, the Marlowes, faced a number of problems. The shopping environment in the Marlowes was uninviting with four lanes of traffic, cluttered pavements and a drab appearance.

The development of the covered Marlowes Shopping Centre in 1990 shifted the primary shopping area away from the main street and significantly increased the level of available retail floorspace. In addition, major developments in competing centres and out-of-town shopping schemes significantly increased competition. As a result vacancies more than doubled in the town centre during the recession in the early 1990s.

The Scheme

The pedestrianisation, environmental improvements and new traffic management arrangements were implemented in three phases, between 1992 and 1994.

Phase 1 involved the re-alignment and re-paving of Bridge Street and a section of the Marlowes to provide a restricted bus, taxi and cycle precinct. The pedestrianisation of the main section of the Marlowes

The Marlowes, before

The Marlowes, after

was completed as a second phase. Phase 3 involved the re-paving and improvements to the 'ramp' area in the Marlowes. Modernisation of the Market had been in 1991.

The pedestrianisation of the Marlowes created an extensive new public area. This space was fully utilised, accommodating numerous public art features, landscaping, canopies for street trading, an events area, a play area and a new information centre. An area has been retained for disabled car parking at the gateway to the pedestrianised area. More recently pavement cafés have been introduced.

Process and Implementation

The emerging problems faced by Hemel Hempstead were recognised in the mid-1980s. A detailed study of the town centre was commissioned in 1987, which highlighted the potential for pedestrianisation within the Marlowes. A non-statutory Town Centre Plan with a wide range of objectives was prepared in 1988. A number of broad options were considered ranging from the 'do nothing' scenario to full pedestrianisation. Consultation (involving the general public and traders) indicated a high level of support for the pedestrianisation proposals (94% in favour). Further consultation exercises were undertaken during the design stage.

A modern but simple design was considered to be most appropriate for Hemel Hempstead. The durability and suitability of the materials were thoroughly tested prior to selection. The chosen scheme was phased in order to minimise disruption, and work was carefully programmed to avoid the Christmas trade periods.

Management and Maintenance

A maintenance strategy has been adopted, since the scheme was implemented, which attempts to co-ordinate cleaning and maintenance activities within various departments in the district and county councils. The established town centre management initiative in Hemel Hempstead has helped this process. Other management initiatives have supported the pedestrianisation scheme, including CCTV, Shopmobility and promotional exercises.

A comprehensive on-going evaluation programme has been adopted in order to evaluate the progress and benefits of the scheme. Comprehensive before and after surveys (1992 and 1995) and appraisals have been undertaken by consultants.

Evaluation

The comprehensive evaluation of the improvements undertaken in Hemel Hempstead by the Borough Council clearly show strong social benefits. The commercial benefits are less dramatic. However, it appears that the scheme has helped to stabilise the vitality and viability of the town centre during a difficult recessionary period. The future of Hemel Hempstead is now more secure and the town centre is in a strong position to effectively compete with other centres.

Trading Performance
A survey of traders provides a mixed picture with

Public art with a local theme, Hemel Hempstead

regard to trading performance. Car park usage has increased by 18%. It is also important to note that there has been a significant increase in competition from neighbouring towns and out-of-town developments since the scheme was implemented. Therefore, Hemel Hempstead appears to have performed well since the scheme was completed.

Property Investment
Vacancy levels within the Marlowes have remained relatively stable since the scheme was completed. However, a parade of shop units within the pedestrianised area has recently been purchased and are being refurbished to provide modern accommodation, which should reduce vacancies in the near future.

Property Values
Rental levels and capital values have fallen in Hemel Hempstead between 1992-1995. However, similar reductions have been experienced within neighbouring towns. Therefore, it would appear that Hemel Hempstead has maintained its position within the hierarchy despite increasing competition.

Awards
Town Centre Environment Award 1995 – British Council of Shopping Centres

Noise and Pollution
Actual air quality and noise readings within the pedestrianisation area show a significant improvement since the scheme was implemented.

Social Benefits
A survey of shoppers demonstrates that the measures undertaken have led to a perceived improvement in; the quality of the shopping environment, the provision of places to sit and rest, disabled access and security within the shopping area and car parks. Inevitably pedestrianisation has led to a perceived reduction in accessibility by public transport.

ILFORD – SELECTIVE PEDESTRIANISATION

THE GOOD PRACTICE CASE

The development of the town relief road and pedestrianisation of Ilford's core shopping areas has helped to retain the town centre as a major shopping destination within north east London, and has reversed the decline experienced during the 1970's. The scheme has acted as a catalyst to secure £125 million of private sector investment, including the development of a major new covered shopping centre.

The extent of the pedestrianised area was limited to only half of the primary shopping street, following careful considered and extensive consultation. This pedestrianised section contains the main comparison retailers who benefit most from window shopping. The retention of vehicular access in other sections of the street has allowed a high level of accessibility to be retained. It has benefited businesses who require vehicular access for passing trade. Further measures to retain accessibility have been very successful. Pedestrian access to neighbouring residential areas cut off by the new relief road has been ensured by the provision of safe and well maintained underpasses. New car parks with easy access from the relief road have also helped to minimise the impact on accessibility.

Key Issues
High Road, the primary shopping street within Ilford town centre, accommodated four lanes of heavy traffic. Congestion and pedestrian/ vehicular conflict was severe, particularly at the numerous side street junctions on to High Road. The town centre experienced considerable decline during the 1970's, losing several major retailers and department stores. The removal or reduction of traffic was a priority.

The Scheme
A town centre relief road, Winston Way, was completed in 1985. This road diverted through traffic to the south of Ilford town centre, and allowed the High Road to be closed and pedestrianised.

The middle section of the High Road was pedestrianised in 1988. Servicing is still permitted during restricted hours and improvements to rear servicing have been undertaken. Bus and taxi access has been provided at the western end of the High Road.

Modern materials and designs have been used, appropriate to the character of the town centre.

Ilford High Road

Retained access for service and maintenance

Process and Implementation

The problems of decline during the 1970's led to an evaluation of the town centre. Initially, the option to provide a full town centre ring road was considered, which may have enabled wider pedestrianisation. However, this solution was considered to be too expensive. As a result the town relief road was implemented.

Proposals to pedestrianise the High Road were subject to considerable consultation and debate, particularly with the bus companies who wanted to retain bus access along the entire street. A town centre committee with representatives from local interest groups were also involved. Following this consultation a compromise was prepared and a reduced pedestrianised section was proposed.

The overall plan was the subject of a comprehensive public inquiry. Designs were exhibited in public within the town centre.

The urban space enhancements were designed within strict budgetary constraints. As a result medium quality materials were used, appropriate to the character of Ilford.

The role of the project team during the implementation of the scheme was critical in minimising disruption and keeping affected parties informed. A single point of contact was essential.

Management and Maintenance

The on-going maintenance and management of the pedestrianised area was considered carefully during the planning stages and material selection. However, the Ilford experience has highlighted the problems of funding cleaning and maintenance on an annual basis. Political pressures and other priorities can impact on future funding. Ideally, a dedicated budget to fund maintenance and repairs through the lifecycle of the scheme would be most appropriate.

Evaluation

Ilford town centre has performed remarkably well during the recession, despite the impact of the Lakeside Shopping Centre at Thurrock which has affected many centres within East London. The pedestrianised area appears to be buoyant. However, the non-pedestrianised peripheral shopping areas have to some extent declined. The Borough Council have recognised that the role of these secondary areas will change and that alternative uses may need to be permitted, including leisure and entertainment.

Trading Performance
PMRS pedestrian flowcounts indicate an increase in weekly flows in both the pedestrianised and unpedestrianised sections of the High Road between 1987 and 1994, although this will be partly due to the opening of the Exchange Centre. Pedestrian flows in secondary shopping areas have remained relatively stable.

Property Investment
The implementation of pedestrianisation in the High Road was a key factor in securing the development of the Exchange Shopping Centre a 300,000 sq. ft development which open three years after pedestrianisation was completed.

Vacancy levels within the pedestrianised area have remained very low throughout the recession despite the opening of the Exchange and Lakeside Thurrock. However, vacancies in other areas have increased in line with the national trend during the recession.

Property Values
Prime pitch zone A rental levels increased in Ilford during the worst part of the recession, and remain at around £100 per sq. ft.

Safety & Security
Having undertaken a business crime audit in conjunction with the Police and the British Retail Consortium, the introduction of CCTV was seen as a major priority. A successful bid for matched funding was made to the Home Office. CCTV has helped to reduce vandalism by around 50%.

Social Benefits
A survey of shoppers in Ilford in 1995 indicated that 59% of respondents rated the town centre as very good or excellent, and had improved significantly from previous surveys (43% in 1990). Only 3% rated Ilford as being poor.

KILMARNOCK – LONG TERM ENHANCEMENT

THE GOOD PRACTICE CASE

A long term approach to the enhancement, management and maintenance of the urban spaces has been adopted in Kilmarnock. The measures implemented have not compromised on quality, durability or coverage. The extended lifespan, perhaps over 100 years, of the scheme should off-set the initial high capital cost (approximately £7.5 million). The use of natural materials has produced an attractive streetscape and has enhanced civic pride and business confidence in the town.

Regeneration of the town centre is part of a holistic economic regeneration strategy for East Ayrshire as a whole. The emphasis on economic regeneration and a strong and close working partnership between the Council and Enterprise Ayrshire were critical to the successful bid for significant European funding. The partnership have put in place structures to effectively evaluate and monitor the improvements.

Key Issues
Industrial decline for many years, particularly in the 1980's, left Kilmarnock with a legacy of high unemployment and a poor environment.

The pedestrianisation areas in the town centre, implemented in the late 1970's, were unattractive expanses of 'black top' and cracked paving. Street furniture and lighting were worn out. The Bus Station also needed a major overhaul. Shoppers were increasingly choosing other centres and business investment was difficult to attract due to the town's poor image. Gap sites had remained undeveloped.

The Cross, before

The Cross, after

Natural granite laid by skilled contractors

The Scheme

The project comprised three elements; town centre street resurfacing, an upgrade of the historic core and the refurbishment of the Bus Station, an important gateway to the town centre.

The streetscape works used a combination of high quality natural stones including granite setts and Caithness sandstone slabs. Uniquely designed cast iron street furniture and lighting along with artwork were commissioned. The surface coverage of the scheme is extensive, including most of the main shopping street (King Street) and many secondary areas.

Process and Implementation

A household survey of local residents and a SWOT analysis of Kilmarnock town centre clearly demonstrated problems of the poor image of the town. Public meetings and consultation with traders indicated that there was a general consensus that improvements were required. A conceptual study of the town centre was prepared.

The initial design proposals were not feasible within the budgetary constraints, a lower quality solution was put forward, but was rejected. The decision not to compromise on quality was taken, and the improvements were delayed. A higher quality solution re-emerged following further consultation and the formation of a partnership between the Council and Ayrshire Enterprise. A bid for European funding was made.

An experienced design team was appointed to undertake design proposals and expert contractors were employed to ensure quality. The scale of the proposals demanded a comprehensive phasing plan. Five stages of work have been implemented over a two year period (1993-1995). Construction was programmed to avoid Christmas periods.

Management and Maintenance

The introduction of natural materials presented new management and cleaning issues. Indeed, a number of problems had to be remedied during the construction of the scheme.

The new surfaces were not ideal for existing cleaning practices and future repairs could be costly. A detailed maintenance manual was adopted following the completion of the scheme, which has provided an appropriate framework to guide the relevant managing bodies. The unification of the regional and district councils and the Town Centre Management Board have improved management co-ordination.

A thorough framework for the economic evaluation of the scheme has also been established. A baseline study was undertaken prior to implementation and a mid-term evaluation has been completed. Further evaluation exercises will be undertaken after 2 years and 4 years to monitor the progress of the scheme.

Evaluation

Given that the scheme was competed less than two years ago, it is in some respects too early to assess the full impact of the improvements. Nevertheless, initial evaluation information indicates that the changes have been very successful in social terms. The scheme has been widely acclaimed for its quality and aesthetic improvement to Kilmarnock town centre. The economic evidence is less conclusive at this stage.

Trading Performance

Surveys of shoppers undertaken before and after the changes were implemented suggest that the frequency of visits to Kilmarnock has improved. Nearly 30% of shoppers suggested that the improvements had encouraged them to visit the town centre more often. Furthermore, 14% of visitors indicated that their expenditure in the town had increased due to the improvements. Although 4% suggested their expenditure reduced during construction works.

The survey of businesses showed a more cautious response. A number of traders indicated that trade had fallen during construction (5% decrease on average). The majority of traders expected this downturn in sales to be short term.

Property Investment

The business survey indicates that over £2.5 million of in-store investment was attributable to the works. The changes to the environmental quality of the street has stimulated improvements to a number of shop frontages.

The environmental improvements have also resulted in a higher quality development on one of the gap sites than would otherwise have been achieved.

Property Values
Zone A rents in Kilmarnock increased slowly between 1993 and 1995, while rents in other nearby centres remained static. Again, it is too early to ascertain the full impact of the changes.

Awards
Nominated for the Royal Town Planning Institute Silver Jubilee Cup
RIAS: Regeneration Award (1995) Bus Station
GIAS Award (1995) Bus Station
Nominated for the Millennium Marquee (Tidy Britain Group)
Nominated for an Association for Business Sponsorship of the Arts

Safety & Security
Survey results show that the changes to the Bus Station have increased shoppers' perception of safety.

Social Benefits
The survey of shoppers in 1995 indicated that only 1% of shoppers believed that the measures had had a negative impact on the town centre. The majority of respondents suggested that there has been a marked improvement. However, 15% (particularly the elderly) had expressed some dislike of the relatively uneven natural stone surfaces.

Dislikes identified before the changes relating to loitering, litter, graffiti and the appearance of the pedestrianised areas were not evident in the 1995 'after' survey.

Over 90% of businesses considered that the changes had been positive.

MARKET HARBOROUGH – SPEED RESTRICTION ZONE

THE GOOD PRACTICE CASE

The benefits of the Market Harborough Bypass have been enhanced by complementary traffic management and environmental measures within the town centre. Market Harborough was selected to join in the National Bypass Demonstration Project organised and partly funded by the Department of Transport. The construction of the bypass has enabled the local authority to implement a range of improvements, which have created a safer and more attractive environment for pedestrians and cyclists.

These measures have given more space to pedestrian and less to motor traffic and have discouraged unnecessary traffic passing though the town centre. A 20 mph speed limit zone has been established through the central area, along with imaginatively designed traffic calming features. More on-street car parking has been provided than existed before the bypass. The scheme has used designs appropriate to the town centre conservation area, including the use of materials that match historic buildings.

Key Issues
Prior to the Market Harborough Bypass approximately 2,200 HGV vehicles passed through the town

Market Harborough, before

Market Harborough, after

centre each day, presenting an unfriendly, congested and relatively unsafe environment for shoppers. The situation was considerably improved by the bypass. However, local traffic, buses and delivery vehicles still passed through the town centre. Further measures were required to slow traffic through the town.

The existing public spaces within the town centre, The Square and Church Square, were relatively poor quality. Several pedestrian links also needed to be improved. The bypass provided the opportunity to enhance the public spaces within the town centre and improve safety and the overall quality of the environment.

The Scheme

A comprehensive traffic management scheme throughout the town centre and surrounding streets was implemented. Environmental improvements, street furniture and bus shelters have been provided, particularly within sensitive areas around the Square, the Old Grammar School and Church. These provided a strong local theme in the use of materials, notably the use of timber features.

A mixture of man-made and natural materials have been used for the pavements and carriageway, with more costly materials used in the most sensitive areas.

The traffic management measures include the introduction of a 20 mph speed limit zone within the town centre, which has been supported by a number of traffic calming and safety measures, such as:

- raised junctions and flat topped road humps;
- contrasting textured and coloured surfaces;
- the introduction of one-way streets;
- narrow, less obtrusive road markings;
- wider pavements and road narrowing;
- lay-bys for parking, buses and loading;
- new pedestrian crossings; and
- segregated cycle tracks.

Process and Implementation

A detailed SWOT analysis and a number of consultation exercises were undertaken for all the bypass demonstration projects. Questionnaire leaflet was used in Market Harborough to obtain the views of the public and trader. Three broad strategy objectives were presented. Given, the sensitivity of the Market Harborough Conservation Area, on-going consultation with English Heritage was vital.

During the planning and implementation of the scheme a number of informative leaflets and newsletters were issued, providing regular updates on the progress of scheme, timetables, disruption and rearrangements.

Management and Maintenance

As part of the Bypass Demonstration Project the benefits of the scheme have been carefully monitored, including public attitude surveys, traffic speed and flow measurements and noise and pollution recordings. In addition, a programme of monitoring surveys has been undertaken by the District Council, including land use and pedestrian flow surveys, which are evaluating the success of the scheme for a number of years.

The Square, Market Harborough

The Old Grammer School, Market Harborough

The Market Harborough Partnership has provided an appropriate platform for managing and maintaining the enhanced public areas within Market Harborough. A code of practice for the on-going maintenance and cleaning has been implemented. The design of the traffic calming measures scheme has aided the successful policing of the scheme.

Evaluation

The removal of bypass traffic has had significant overall benefits in terms of reducing noise, congestion and pollution. The environmental measures have increased space for pedestrians by 22% within the town centre. The ambience of the town centre has been improved by tree planting and new street furniture. The traffic calming measures have reduced average speeds and increased safety and upgraded the environmental quality of the former trunk road.

It is too early to establish the full economic benefits of the scheme. However, recent monitoring shows that the there are encouraging signs for the future, and demonstrate that investment confidence is returning.

Trading Performance
Pedestrian flowcounts suggest that pedestrian activity reduced during the construction period due to disruption. However, pedestrian flows had started to improve following the completion of the scheme, returning to previous levels within the primary shopping area. The continued letting of units within the St Mary's shopping development has been a major success since the implementation of the scheme and vacancy levels throughout the town are relatively low (less than 9%) suggesting that Market Harborough's performance is relatively satisfactory.

Property Investment
Shop vacancies within the town centre have reduced by 40% between June 1994 and June 1996, partly due to lettings within the St Mary's Shopping Centre which was completed in 1993.

Safety & Security
Traffic speeds have been reduced significantly, improving safety in and around the town centre. The traffic calming measures and restrictions have successfully reduced average speeds from over 30 mph to less than 20 mph. Improved pedestrian crossing and dedicated cycle routes have improved safety levels.

Social Benefits
The attitude surveys conducted showed that 67% of respondents believed that the measures had improved overall conditions. Only 24% of respondents suggested that the changes had made Market Harborough's problems worse.
The bypass and traffic calming measures have reduced traffic flows within the town centre a 30-40% reduction, and have significantly reduced congestion.
Noise levels were high before the bypass. The bypass significantly reduced noise levels within the High Street. Further reductions were recorded after the traffic calming measures were introduced. The traffic calming measures have also reduced nitrogen dioxide concentrations within the town centre by between 35-45%.

MORECAMBE – SEAFRONT TERN PROJECT

THE GOOD PRACTICE CASE

The Morecambe TERN project is an excellent example of a specific urban space project to rejuvenate the landward and seaward sides of a jetty. The Stone Jetty is part of the central promenade area of the town centre which can offer considerable attraction to visitors especially during good weather. The TERN project has transformed the area which was a run down neglected eyesore into a focus for public art in a high quality setting.

At the heart of the project has been a commitment to high quality materials, which can withstand the harsh environment, and the involvement of leading designers and artists.
The continuing involvement of all sectors of the community has ensured widespread support for the dramatic change that has already been achieved.

Key Issues
The objectives of the TERN Project were to:

Stone Jetty, Morecambe

- improve the relationship of the jetty with surrounding buildings including the Midland Hotel;

- recognise the inherent potential of the area and generate visitor attractions around the jetty;

- remove obsolete and decaying structures and rationalise the clutter of the amusement area;

- provide a framework to attract new investment to meet the needs of residents and visitors; and

- create a stronger relationship with the sea by improving the Stone Jetty and to introduce a more sheltered environment for visitors.

The Scheme

Within the context of Lancaster City Council's intention to remodel the seafront, the improvements around the Stone Jetty have become a key visual attraction. The strategy as set out in the development brief for the central promenade redevelopment area (1993) envisaged new development opportunities in the area as well as its continued role as an important public open space and a location for high volume leisure facilities.

The revitalisation of the Stone Jetty, with its range of public art exhibits provides a new destination for visitors which will help to generate higher levels of pedestrian flow in the area. The jetty is provided with an attractive tea room, lavatories and seating areas which complement the surrounding uses and provide shelter for visitors as well as resting areas. An extension of this strategy to approach roads and roundabouts has helped to link new developments, the existing town and the seafront. Further work is planned along the seafront adjacent to Morecambe town centre.

Process and Implementation

In the late 1980's, there was a growing recognition that Morecambe's traditional tourist attractions were losing their appeal. In January 1989, Lancaster City Council produced a discussion paper designed to lead to a renaissance of the resort. As part of the local plan process a development brief was published outlining proposals for the area.

The council helped to facilitate a consultative network involving residents, local businesses, public bodies and other interest groups. A series of working groups has been established to take forward key elements of the strategy (e.g. funding, design, publicity, management). Council officers and members sit on these groups and the council receives regular reports from each of them.

Design competitions have been adopted as the preferred mechanism to achieve high quality and innovation. Lists of recognised artists in a wide variety of materials have been assembled and evaluated as part of this process.

Funding has come from many sources. Initially, coastal protection works provided the opportunity to finance public works of art. More recently, derelict land grant and single regeneration budget have also contributed to the scheme. Investment has also come from the private sector, notably Morrisons food stores in the form of planning gain associated with the development of their new superstore adjacent to the jetty. The council has played an enabling role both by creating a specific fund for public art and by identifying alternative construction methods which incorporate works of art and high quality infrastructure materials at no extra cost.

Management and Maintenance

The management costs of the existing tourist attractions (e.g. promenade lights) were often relatively high. In many cases it has been possible to replace the existing attractions with new public works of art and, because of their durability, to effect a reduction in maintenance costs.

Evaluation

The TERN project has successfully introduced public art and street furniture through public and private sector contributions and has made a major contribution to the public domain.

The major programme of site clearance, redevelopment and, especially, the introduction of a substantial amount of high quality public art has had a significant impact on the quality of the environment. Early indications are of an increase in the number of visitors to the area.

Property Investment
The new Morrisons food store is a clear indication of the private sectors commitment to the scheme.

Awards
British Gas Street Lighting Award

PETERSFIELD – TOWN CENTRE GATEWAY IMPROVEMENTS

THE GOOD PRACTICE CASE

Access to Petersfield's small market town centre was hindered by congestion caused by trunk road through traffic. Petersfield's inclusion within the Department of Transport's Bypass Demonstration Project offered a solution to this problem. However, the removal of trunk road traffic on to the A3 bypass presented new challenges. Petersfield has maximised the environmental and social benefits that the bypass has brought.

The old route on the periphery of the town centre has been successfully transformed from an unattractive trunk road carriageway into a pleasant, functional and safe gateway into the town centre. The requirements of pedestrians, traffic entering the town centre and cross-town traffic have been balanced through careful design. The implemented junction design has taken the opportunity to modify drivers' behaviour, reducing speeds but maintaining accessibility. The scheme has cleverly used tactile materials to avoid the excessive use of road markings, bollards, chicanes and ramps. Furthermore, appropriate materials, in-keeping with the historic characteristics of the Petersfield Conservation Area, have been used.

Key Issues

The removal of trunk road traffic from the old A3 route left Petersfield with an unattractive and pedestrian unfriendly approach into the town centre. In some respects the less congested road looked more unattractive than it had been with heavy traffic. The carriageways, road markings and trunk road standard lighting were an inappropriate gateway to an attractive market town. The reduced traffic in the street offered opportunities for speeding.

The route remains an important cross-town route for local traffic and the main route into the town centre, which ruled out the closure or restrictions to vehicular access.

Petersfield, before

Petersfield, after

The Scheme

Dragon Street, formally part of the A3, has been completely rebuilt. Reduced traffic since the bypass has allowed the carriageways to be narrowed from 7-13 metres to 5.5 metres. Channels or overrun areas in contrasting materials have helped to make the carriageway look narrower, slowing traffic further. Pavements have been widened and re-paved. Planting, parking bays and bus stops have been provided. Junctions have been treated with raised block paving to provide a 'gateway' effect. Sensitively designed and co-ordinated street furniture, lighting and signs were installed.

Process and Implementation

Clear management structures were set up for the implementation of all bypass demonstrations, which provided formal linkages between the local authorities (county, district and town councils), the Department of Transport and local interest groups.

A joint officers working party was in existence before bids were made to the DoT, and an action plan recognising the problems faced by Petersfield was in place. This joint working and action plan enabled Petersfield to submit a co-ordinated and comprehensive bid to the DoT within a short timetable.

The officer working party was a multi-disciplinary team, reporting to the project steering group and the joint district and county council members panel. The success of the proposals was also underpinned by guidance from a Town Forum which represented local interests. A marketing panel was also established to address potential loss of trade due to the bypass and disruption during construction.

An initial public meeting generated a positive response to the environmental improvements. Further consultation during the planning stages consisted of two comprehensive attitude surveys undertaken as part of the Demonstration Project, and public exhibitions demonstrating proposed designs. The designs were modified on a number of occasions following feedback during the process.

Management and Maintenance

Close working between the county and district council and the formation of the town centre forum have ensured a committed and co-ordinated approach to the on-going management of the scheme and the town centre in general.

Monitoring the scheme, as part of the Bypass Demonstration Project, was undertaken at three stages, two prior to implementation and one after, which included:

- measures of traffic flows and speed;
- pedestrian movements;
- noise and air quality readings; and
- attitude surveys for pedestrians, cyclists, residents and businesses.

Evaluation

The removal of bypass traffic has had significant overall benefits in terms of reducing noise, congestion and pollution. Journey times into the town centre have also been improved. The traffic calming measures have reduced average speeds and increased safety and upgraded the environmental quality of the former trunk road.

Traffic calming measures

High quality street furniture

Trading Performance
Petersfield is a successful market town which has performed better than many similar towns during the recession. Therefore, it is difficult to identify a marked improvement in performance since the completion of the bypass and environmental improvements. Nevertheless, the letting of units within the Ram Walk shopping development has been a major success since the implementation of the scheme and vacancy levels throughout the town are relatively low suggesting that Petersfield is in a healthy state.

Property Investment
The scheme has helped to instil civic pride. Noticeably properties in the street are being better looked after. A number of shops have been re-painted since the scheme was implemented.

Traffic Flows
Traffic flows have reduced by two thirds since the bypass was built. In addition, accessibility into the town centre was significantly improved, with average journey times decreasing by 10-28%.

Safety & Security
The removal of traffic on to the bypass initially increased average speeds along Dragon Street and College Street. However, the implementation of the environmental measures has reduced speeds and reduced accidents.

Noise and Air Quality
Before and after surveys show a marked reduction in noise levels. Significant reductions (over 40%) in nitrogen dioxide concentrations were achieved.

Social Benefits
The attitude surveys conducted showed that 67% of respondents believed that the measures had improved overall conditions. The scheme has provided more space for the pedestrian and cyclist, and has greatly improved the overall environmental quality whilst boosting civic pride.

SOLIHULL – ENHANCEMENT AND MANAGEMENT INITIATIVES

THE GOOD PRACTICE CASE

The creation of a structured Town Centre Management Initiative in Solihull has ensured that the benefits of pedestrianisation and environmental improvements have been maximised. A comprehensive programme of management measures has been implemented or is currently proposed to secure the on-going success of the town centre.

Improvement works to rear servicing roads enabled the implementation of pedestrianisation and urban space enhancement within the High Street. The use of natural materials in sensitive areas and man-made materials elsewhere have provided good value for money.

Key Issues
The High Street in Solihull was narrow and suffered from congestion and pollution. Its road safety record was a major concern. The town also faced a number of threats including; the effects of the recession, out-of-town retail developments and increasing competition from neighbouring towns.

The council feared that the town centre would decline rapidly if measures to improve the general attraction of Solihull were not implemented. A strategy for the enhancement and future management of Solihull town centre was seen as the appropriate response. Traders within the High Street had been against pedestrianisation in the past. However, a re-appraisal by the Council established broad public and business support.

The High Street, Solihull

The High Street, Solihull

The Scheme
Solihull High Street was closed to traffic and pedestrianised in 1994. Man-made brick pavers and slabs were used predominantly. However, natural York stone was used in the most sensitive areas, particularly near Listed buildings.

Improvements to rear access routes have enabled full vehicular restrictions to be implemented. Decorative street furniture and public art have been provided, which reflect the historic character of the streetscape. Traffic calming measures, dedicated disabled parking spaces and re-arranged bus stops have been provided to ensure safe and convenient pedestrian access to the High Street.

Process and Implementation
A number of broad options were considered ranging from full road closure and pedestrianisation, restricted access for buses and the disabled, pavement widening through to environmental refurbishment works only.

Following initial consultation, visits to other schemes and detailed evaluation, the full pedestrianisation scheme was identified as the most practical and beneficial solution. Design consultants were commissioned to prepare broad concept designs. These concepts were taken forward by a multi-disciplinary team of council officers. Working within a tight budgetary constraint led to the selective use of natural materials.

Management and Maintenance
The pedestrianisation and environmental improvements implemented in Solihull were not considered on their own to be sufficient to secure the future vitality of the town centre. The Borough Council recognised that the town centre needed to be treated as a special case, and that its future maintenance and cleaning requirements could not be incorporated wholly within the council's highways duties.

A co-ordinated partnership approach to the town centre was needed. The need for a committed and co-ordinated approach led to the formation of a Town Centre Management Group within the council and the appointment of a Town Centre Co-ordinator. This group was established to improve dialogue between the council, retailers and other town centre interests and to more effectively market and promote the town centre.

A number of management measures has been implemented since the pedestrianisation scheme was completed, which has helped to maximise the potential of new urban spaces created by the scheme, including:

- Radio link and CCTV;
- a Shopmobility scheme;
- Code of Practice for entertainers and advertising boards;
- special Events including Christmas Entertainment;
- improved cleanliness and maintenance monitoring;
- a pavement Cafe initiative;
- customer surveys; and
- training programmes.

Further plans include the formation of a Town Centre Steering Group linking public and private sector interests and the production of a shared vision statement and a Town Centre Business plan.

Evaluation
The environmental and management measures undertaken in Solihull have been widely viewed as successful, both in social and commercial terms. Solihull appears to be vibrant despite increasing competition from neighbouring centres and out-of-town developments.

Trading Performance
A 10% increase in the use of town centre car parks in Solihull is an early sign of the success of the scheme in attracting higher numbers of shoppers.

Property Investment
Solihull has not suffered from high levels of shop vacancies during the recession in comparison to other centres, particularly within the High Street. However, there has been a marginal reduction in the number of vacancies in Solihull since the early 1990's.

A number of major operators have extended or reinvested in their stores in Solihull since the improvements, including Marks and Spencer, WH Smith, Beatties and BHS. Proposals for the £90 million development of a 300,000 sq. ft shopping mall are also progressing.

Property Values
Rental levels in Solihull were extremely high during the boom of the late 1980's, but fell dramatically during the recession. Prime pitch zone A rental levels fell by over a third between 1990 and 1993, but have started to improve since the pedestrianisation of the High Street. Rents improved by 10% between 1993 and 1996 to around £95 per sq. ft.

Safety & Security
The accident problem within the High Street has been eliminated, and Solihull Police have reported that the introduction of CCTV and radio link systems have resulted in a significant increase in arrests.

Social Benefits
The creation of an improved shopping environment has proved to be almost universally popular based on comments received by the council. There has been a considerable increase in street activity and promotional events. However, the success of the scheme has introduced new challenges to the management team, particularly with regard to the control of street trading, buskers and evening activities.

STOWMARKET – MARKET TOWN IMPROVEMENTS

THE GOOD PRACTICE CASE

The introduction of traffic management and pedestrian priority measures in Stowmarket was thoroughly tested and amended accordingly before implementation. Comprehensive consultation and experimental measures ensured that a viable solution was identified. The scheme has retained an appropriate balance between vehicular accessibility and the requirements of the pedestrian. It is a good example of an effective pedestrian priority area within the core of a small historic market town.

The development of a major out-of-town retail scheme has had a major impact on the town centre. The improvements may help the town respond to increasing competition. The implementation of the scheme has been instrumental in the formation of a more co-ordinated approach to the management of Stowmarket town centre.

The Market Place, Stowmarket

Key Issues
Stowmarket is an attractive small market town. The linear shopping area, Ipswich Street and Bury Street, accommodated two lanes of traffic providing only narrow pavements for pedestrian. Through traffic, service vehicles and illegal parking created a congested and relatively unsafe environment for shoppers, and the Market Place was cramped.

The development of the Inner Relief Road in 1992 removed through traffic from the town centre. The new road also provided opportunities to improve the shopping environment and the extension of the Market Place. However, the need to retain accessibility and servicing arrangements was a major obstacle which had to be overcome.

The Scheme
A pedestrian priority scheme and one-way traffic system have been implemented within the primary shopping area of Ipswich Street, the Market Place and a section of Bury Street. These traffic arrangements have allowed pavements to be widened, creating more

Pedestrian priority, Ipswich Street

Traffic calming measures, Ipswich Street

space for street furniture, planting (semi-mature trees) and an enlarged market. Dedicated lay-bys have been provided for buses, service vehicles and taxis.

Traffic calming measures and regular pedestrian crossing points have been provided to improve safety. The pedestrian areas have been clearly defined using light coloured slabs. The carriageway and lay-bys have been laid with darker brick pavers. The scheme was implemented in two phases during 1993 and 1994.

Process and Implementation

Trunk road through traffic was removed from Stowmarket town centre after the A45 bypass was completed in the early 1970's. However, considerable local through traffic continued to pass through the town centre. The council used capital receipts from land sales to finance the construction of a much needed Inner Relief Road in 1992.

Proposals to remove traffic and improve the environment for shoppers were exhibited prior to the completion of the Inner Relief Road, highlighting a high level of support from the general public. A study was also commissioned to look at the potential for improving the town centre. This report confirmed the need to undertake the proposed improvement in order to counter the impact of proposed out-of-town retail developments.

The removal of all vehicular traffic from Ipswich Street and Bury Street to provide a pedestrianised area was not feasible due to servicing arrangements. It was also unsatisfactory in terms of bus access. Experimental arrangements restricting access to buses, taxis, deliveries and private permit holders were implemented. However, the large number of access permits issued made the scheme impractical and difficult to police.

A multi-disciplinary officer working group was established with representatives from the district and county councils, reporting to a joint members panel. Consultation with local traders and interest groups was undertaken throughout the process. A Steering Group representing traders, the bus and taxi companies, the Police, landowners and council officers met on a regular basis.

There was some level of apprehension amongst retailers who feared the scheme would lead to a loss in trade. The scheme was undertaken in two phases in order to minimise disruption and work was programmed to avoid the Christmas period.

Management and Maintenance

The responsibilities for maintenance and cleaning have remained with the county and district councils respectively. However, joint working during the planning and implementation of the scheme has led to a more co-ordinated approach to these activities, and an appropriate on-going policy has been adopted. The Consultation process also led to the formation of a local chamber of commerce within Stowmarket.

Evaluation

The scheme has been generally well received by the public, and has significantly improved safety and the environment in the town centre. The economic benefits of the scheme are more difficult to assess, due to the development of a 40,000 sq. ft Tesco out-of-town superstore shortly after the scheme was completed.

The expansion of public spaces has also allowed the twice weekly market to be increased in size.

Trading Performance
Car park usage is stable despite the out-of-town shopping development in 1995, although some traders have suggested that the loss of car parking in the shopping area has impacted on their trading performance.

Property Investment
Vacancy levels within the primary retail area have remained relatively static since the scheme was implemented. However, part of the secondary shopping areas remains fragile due to the effects of the recession and the development of the out-of-town food store.

Safety & Security
No recorded serious or slight accidents have occurred in Ipswich Street since the scheme was implemented. On average there were 3-4 accidents per annum prior to the scheme.

Social Benefits
The changes have clearly improved the environmental quality of Stowmarket's mediaeval core. The provision of extra space for pedestrians has provided opportunities for promotions and events. However, car parking and accessibility may need to be re-addressed.

WINDSOR – HISTORIC CORE ENHANCEMENT

THE GOOD PRACTICE CASE

The implementation of pedestrianisation and urban space enhancement measures has been used in Windsor to re-establish the main commercial area's historical connections. The Royal Borough's overall objective was to secure investment in the future development and promotion of Windsor's historic core and to provide a safer, cleaner and more attractive environment.

The enhancement scheme and management measures demonstrate how the requirements of the pedestrian can be carefully balanced with commercial interests, whilst maintaining quality accessibility. The implementation procedures provide a suitable example of good practice in terms of consultation, contract management and construction/design detail. The emphasis on quality and avoidance of the use of barriers or bollards have ensured that the scheme is in keeping with the historic core and provides an environment suitable for a major tourist destination.

Key Issues
Peascod Street, the primary retail area, is, in places, only 12 metres wide, and had very narrow pavements to accommodate large numbers of shoppers and tourist visitors. The street had significant vehicular traffic flows. As a result the environment was congested, noisy, dangerous and unpleasant for pedestrians. The removal of unnecessary traffic was seen as a priority.

The Scheme
The joint Borough and County Council scheme involved four main elements:

- the pedestrianisation of the primary retail area, Peascod Street;

- pavement widening at the lower end of Peascod Street; and

- traffic calming measures on the periphery, i.e. within Thames Street and High Street improving pedestrian access from Windsor Castle; and

- new bus stop, taxi and disabled parking arrangements around the pedestrianised area.

Essential vehicular access to Peascod Street has been secured by introducing limited access for service vehicles and permit holders outside the main shopping hours (11 am to 4 p.m.) within the pedestrianised area, along with the other traffic management measures highlighted above. A service access route has been maintained along Peascod Street and dedicated loaded bays have been provided. The service route and bays have been defined using a mixture of dark paving materials. Public focal points for seating, public art and street entertainment have also been incorporated. Traffic speeds along the defined service route have been controlled by the careful siting of street furniture.

Peascod Street, Windsor

Street Entertainment, Peascod Street

Process and Implementation

The pedestrianisation of Peascod Street had been considered desirable for a number of years. However, many traders and local people believed that pedestrianisation would be too difficult to implement for access reasons. Many strategic options, such as pavement widening or full pedestrianisation were ruled out due to the limited width of Peascod Street and on-going service requirements. An initial consultation exercise (leaflet and questionnaire) in 1990 indicated wide support for a move towards pedestrianisation (77% in favour). The outline concept was endorsed during the District Local Plan process and a detailed transport study. Potential solutions, within clearly identified physical parameters, were sought via an organised design competition, and consultants were subsequently appointed.

The winning design proposals evolved and were modified by the Design Team (council officers and consultants). This team worked closely with trader and heritage groups, the police and bus operators. Careful consideration was given to the balance between quality and budgetary constraints. A range of cost projections were produced for design/material options. A mixture of natural and high quality man made materials were chosen, which reduced costs but maintained quality and durability.

A second phase of public consultation was undertaken following the production of detailed designs, including another leaflet and questionnaire and a 'roadshow'. Many design elements were fully 'road' tested prior to implementation, for example disabled access, junction design and traffic calming measures. The appointment of a Client Liaison Officer providing a central point of contact within the council was critical to the successful implementation of the scheme. Regular feedback to traders and the public throughout the process helped to minimise disruption and uncertainty.

Management and Maintenance

The on-going management and maintenance of the scheme has been underpinned by:

- the preparation of a detailed maintenance manual;
- a stockpile of replacement materials;
- a policy to control and manage street entertainment;
- a special budgetary provision for on-going maintenance and cleaning; and
- the introduction of CCTV.

However, the creation of public focal points has successfully attracted street entertainers, which has presented a new management problem. Tighter controls are now required to organise and manage street activity.

Evaluation

Despite problems during the implementation of the pedestrianisation and enhancement proposals, there are now encouraging signs for the future.

Trading Performance

The results of a Chamber of Commerce survey of traders conducted shortly after the scheme was completed were inconclusive. Views on the impact of the scheme on trading levels were divided. However, only 30% of the traders suggested that their takings had decreased during the previous year. Disruption during the implementation of the scheme was cited as the main cause for trading reductions. Many of the traditional 'window shopping' businesses, such as clothing, gifts and speciality shops, indicated that their trade had improved. Most traders (over 75%) were optimistic about the future health of Windsor. Highway authority surveys show that pedestrian flows have improved.

Property Investment
Shop vacancies in Windsor have improved since the scheme was implemented, although vacant units within Peascod Street increased during construction works, but have subsequently reduced to just two. Vacancies in Lower Peascod Street have also fallen. The improvements have also acted as catalyst for investment, notably the refurbishment and extension of the Daniel department store. Proposals are also emerging to redevelop the station area (65,000 sq. ft of retail and other facilities) and King Edward's Court shopping centre.

Awards
The recently completed improvements have been submitted for several awards, and won a Special Landscape Category in Britain in Bloom Southern Region.

Property Values
Rental levels in Peascod Street fell during the implementation of the scheme but have improved (£75 to £85 per sq. ft) since the scheme was completed.

Safety and Security
Increased pedestrian safety in the historic core has been achieved through a combination of road humps, widening foot paths, and restricting traffic flow.

Social Benefits
The survey of traders indicated that the principle benefit of the pedestrainisation scheme has been the improvement to the shopping environment. The reduction in congestion and improved pedestrian flow were also cited as principle benefits of the scheme. The creation of new public spaces has been visibly successful in terms of the use of street furniture and street entertainment. Traffic studies indicate that the improvements have reduced car journeys within Windsor. Car trips around town have been reduced by a third and road safety has improved.

WORCESTER – CITY CENTRE REDEVELOPMENT

THE GOOD PRACTICE CASE

Infill development and refurbishment have enabled Worcester to respond to increasing retail competition. These major investments have been carefully and sympathetically integrated into the historic city centre. The development of the CrownGate shopping centre has created new pedestrian links that have improved overall level of permeability throughout the city centre. The scheme has also upgraded existing shopping streets providing new public spaces.

The CrownGate redevelopment exemplifies a fully co-ordinated approach to city centre planning that has ensured the City's future viability. Worcester has attracted more visitors to the town by tackling problems of traffic, cleanliness, security and commercial decline. The genuine partnership approach between the local authority and the developer broadened expectations and resulted in a scheme that achieved far more than was initially envisaged.

Key Issues
During the 1980's, major shopping schemes were being developed or proposed in competing centres. Worcester needed to respond to this increasing competition and out-of-town developments in order to maintain its position within the region.

The historic core suffered from a number of problems, including:

- fragmentation and a lack of cohesion;
- poor permeability due to a lack of pedestrian routes;
- bus and traffic congestion in narrow streets; and
- the 1960's Blackfriars Square shopping centre in need of refurbishment.

Pedestrians linkages into CrownGate

The Scheme

The CrownGate shopping centre was completed in 1992. This development and wider strategy involved the:

- development of under-utilised land;
- redevelopment and refurbishment of the Blackfriars shopping centre;
- a new bus station;
- improved car parking facilities;
- restoration of listed buildings;
- archaeological investigations;
- pedestrianisation and pedestrian priority schemes; and
- a permanent outdoor market.

Process and Implementation

Proposals to redevelop the Blackfriars centre emerged during the late 1970's as pressure from retailers for large premises increased. However, redevelopment of the centre was economically marginal due to the it's peripheral location. These problems prompted the developer and the City Council to undertake a feasibility study for a scheme containing new build on land to the rear of the High Street in order to finance the Blackfriars refurbishment and the development of a new bus station. The enlarged scheme required a partnership approach and Compulsory Purchase Orders to be secured.

A shopping study was undertaken in 1982 which demonstrated that Worcester's catchment population could support the proposed CrownGate development. A draft strategy for the city centre was prepared and incorporated into Local Plan policies in 1985.

By negotiation, team working and public consultation, the council and developer saw new possibilities in the scheme. The scheme was broadened to include new traffic management arrangements, enhanced public spaces and new pedestrian routes. The development proposals were finally granted planning permission in 1989 following a public inquiry.

Management and Maintenance

The success of the package of improvements has been monitored by the City Council, through the production of annual retail monitors. The creation of new pedestrian routes through the Crown Gate has been effectively managed to provide 24 hour access on many routes. Special pedestrian access agreements have ensured permeability. The scheme has also significantly improved servicing arrangements within the historic core, through the adoption of traffic management arrangements. A shopmobility scheme and CCTV linked to the CrownGate centre have helped to improve accessibility and safety.

Careful integration of the CrownGate Centre

Evaluation

The package of proposals implemented in Worcester has had a major impact on the city centre. The individual benefits of specific elements of the overall strategy are difficult to isolate. Nevertheless, the CrownGate development and other improvements have been widely considered to be successful and have enhanced Worcester's position in the regional shopping hierarchy.

The comprehensive package of traffic management measures has given pedestrians priority in a greater area within the city centre. The scheme has provided direct pedestrian links to the High Street and has created new routes connecting formerly isolated areas. It has also enabled a new Heritage Trail to be established through the city centre.

Trading Performance

Pedestrian counts undertaken since the CrownGate opened indicate a considerable increase in the number of shoppers in the newly pedestrianised and enhanced areas (Broad Street and Angel Place). Information from major tenants within the CrownGate scheme also indicate that Worcester's catchment area has increased.

Property Investment

CrownGate centre has been successful in attracting major multiple retailers, including British Home Stores, C&A and Beatties. Elsewhere, investment in the form of store upgrades has been undertaken including Marks and Spencer, Woolworth, Littlewoods and Debenhams.

Overall shop unit vacancy rates in Worcester City Centre declined from 17.5% in 1993 to 14% in 1995, due to the successful letting of the CrownGate centre.

Property Values

Prime pitch Zone A rentals declined by approximately 20% between 1990 and 1992, and have subsequently stabilised. Since the opening of the CrownGate centre rental levels have picked up.

Awards

Town Centre Environment Award 1994 – BCSC
Environment Award 1994 – Business Commitment to the Environment
Urban Renewal Award – Royal Institute of Chartered Surveyors
AA Car Park Safety Certificate
British Archaeological Awards 1989 – Virgin Group

Social Benefits

The city centre strategy has provided a number of social benefits, including; an improved range and quality of shops, better pedestrian linkages, a new out-door market, better and safer shopping, less congestion and a new bus station.

SELECTED BIBLIOGRAPHY

Appleyard, D. *Liveable Streets* (University of California Press 1981)

The Association of Town Centre Management, *Advice Centre* (1994)

The Association of Town Centre Management, *The Effectiveness of Town Centre Management* (1994)

Departments of Landscape and Geography, The University of Sheffield, *Breaking the Downward Spiral: Current and Future Responses of Children to Their Town Centre* (1996)

Design Council and the Royal Town Planning Institute Streets Ahead (Design Council 1979)

DoE, *Greening the City: A Guide to Good Practice* (HMSO 1996)

DoE, *Vital and Viable Town Centres: Meeting the Challenge* (HMSO 1994)

DoT, *Better Places Through Bypasses: Report of the Bypass Demonstration Project* (HMSO 1995)

Environ Best Practice Research Unit, *Paved With Gold?* (Environ Research Report No.7 1992)

Colliers Erdman Lewis Research & Consultancy, *The Pedestrianisation Myth* (1994)

Falk, N. *Successful Public Places: Going From Vision to Results* (Report for the natural and built environment professions – May 1995: No.4)

Gehl, J. *Life Between Buildings: Using Public Space* (Von Nostrand Reinhold Company, New York 1987)

Hass-Klau, C. *The Pedestrian and City Traffic* (Belhaven Press 1990)

Hass-Klau, C. *Streets as Living Space* (Proceedings of the 22nd European Transport Forum 1994)

Pedestrians Association, *Our Kind of Town* (1993)

Roberts, J. *Pedestrian Precincts in Britain* (TEST 1981)

Roberts, J. Quality Streets: *How Traditional Urban Centres Benefit From Traffic Calming* (Transport and Environmental Studies 1992)

Smith, James, *Pedestrianisation – Shopping Streets in Scotland* (The Planner May 1985)

Vernez Moudon, A. (Ed) *Public Streets for Public Use* (Van Rostrand Reinhold 1987)

Printed in the United Kingdom for The Stationery Office.
N0021046, 6/97, C16, 3400, 5673.